ADVANCE PRAISE FOR THE BOOK

'As a former consultant myself, I can relate to this book perfectly.
A consultant's skills are shaped through their experiences with clients and,
over time, they hone their ability to not just find the right answers but
also get their clients to accept and implement them. Sandeep Krishnan has
done a great job of capturing the skills needed to be a good consultant and
the tools to be used, explained through the career of Samanta Thomas.
would be a worthwhile read for anyone aspiring to succeed in the
profession'—G.V. Ravishankar, managing director, Sequoia Capital, and
former consultant, McKinsey & Company

er the past decade, Sandeep Krishnan has provided valuable consulting
ghts to the Manappuram Group. This book showcases his vast
sulting experience backed by deep introspection. It is an absorbing read.
uld recommend it as a ready reckoner for professionals who want to
make an impact and a difference'—V.P. Nandakumar, chairman and
ging director, Manappuram Group

world of consulting beckons some of our best minds. In *The Mind of a
ltant*, Sandeep Krishnan gives us a clear picture of what the practice
sulting is all about. This book should attract wide interest from
onals across the business world'—Professor Rishikesha Krishnan,
IIM Bangalore

ing as a profession pushes you to excel in functional skills and
effectiveness. This book is a great narrative on how to develop
age a consulting mind. Sandeep Krishnan has translated his rich
e into an engaging read. Read it to enhance your professional
—Mervyn Raphael, managing partner, People Business

lting world is a complex high-energy web of various skills. Yet
the best places to learn and build one's legacy. Every day in
is a "new opportunity". Those who can embrace this spirit
rong professionals. Sandeep Krishnan has brought his learnings
very readable book. This is clearly a book for everybody in the
world!'—Alpana Dutta, partner, Ernst & Young India.

wn Sandeep Krishnan from his days as a student in IIM
He has encapsulated the rich insights of working with various
book. I am sure it will be a worthwhile read for consultants
usiness professionals alike'—Rakesh Basant, professor,
ad

THE MIND OF A CONSULTAN

a
d
th
It
pr
for

'Ov
insi
cons
I wo
both
mana

'The w
Consu
of con
profess
director

'Consult
personal
and lever
experienc
success!'_

'The consu
it is one o
consulting
emerge as s
together in a
professional

'I have kno
Ahmedabad.
clients in this
and other b
IIM Ahmedab

'*The Mind of a Consultant* contains a wealth of relevant advice that can help any professional in their career. The book effectively captures the career phases of a professional in the consulting world, from the entry level to the designation of a partner. The learning one takes away from that journey is universal and makes for a very interesting read'—Sushanth Tharappan, senior vice president and head, Infosys Leadership Institute

'Sandeep Krishnan has come up with a book that throws light on the life of a business consultant. It is a must-read for anybody who aspires to be in the consulting world or would like to know what goes into making a great consultant. I am sure these skills will be useful for other professionals as well. The icing on the cake is getting to learn all this through the fascinating journey of Samanta Thomas, which makes for a delightful and gripping page-turner'—Kishan Kashyap, coordinator, Consult Club, IIM Ahmedabad, and summer intern, Bain & Company

'*The Mind of a Consultant* is an interesting read that can help one understand the persona of a successful consultant. Sandeep Krishnan presents the discussion on the essential skills of a successful professional through some very compelling storytelling. This is a very well-written book that I really enjoyed reading'—Arvind N. Agrawal, former management board member, RPG Enterprises, and business coach

'After *The Making of a CEO*, Sandeep Krishnan is back with another very interesting book, which captures the important skills a consultant needs to develop to be able to grow in the field. These skills are deep and universal in nature'—Raju Menon, chairman and group managing partner, Kreston Menon Group, Dubai

'This book gives readers a 360-degree view of the business consulting world. From entering a management institute to becoming a partner, *The Mind of a Consultant* gives readers a candid view of the learnings, challenges and skills required for a consultant to be effective in their profession. I find the insights in this book pertinent to professionals across the business world'—Sunil Maheshwari, professor, IIM Ahmedabad

'Sandeep has a wealth of experience in management consulting and, in this book, he has provided an in-depth view of the various phases of a consultant's journey, and the necessary skills and tools. This will be useful for both practising and aspiring consultants'—Georgie Antony, regional director, Asia Pacific, Personnel Search Services, Singapore

'This book is deeply engaging, and I can relate to the learnings described here pertaining to the roles of both internal and external consultants in an organization. *The Mind of a Consultant* brings together the difficult-to-acquire skills that catalyse professional success and a very interesting narrative'—Nishith Mohanty, group president, HR, Manipal Education and Medical Group

'In this book, Sandeep Krishnan has brought to life his rich experience in research and consulting through a compelling storytelling narrative of the capabilities and approaches relevant to a consultant, external or internal. This book is an insightful read for management professionals at any stage in their careers'—Syed Azfar Hussain, senior vice president, human resources, Bajaj Finserv

'This book provides interesting insights into consulting skills that can be valuable to aspiring professionals. Sandeep Krishnan has covered various aspects of the subject with an engaging storyline'—Praveen P.A., director, aerospace, defence and BFSI, Government of Telangana

'Sandeep Krishnan has compiled his vast experience of working with clients from diverse industries into a very engaging book. A consultant has a wide repertoire of skills that can prove valuable in helping clients seek out solutions to challenging business problems. This book is a must for all business professionals and a great read'—Sabyasachi Bhattacharya, executive director, Phillips Carbon Black Limited

'Sandeep Krishnan has deep expertise in the consulting field and has mastered the art of solving organizational challenges. This book delves into skills that matter to professionals so they can make a difference in their respective fields. A must-read!'—Ratish Jha, senior vice president and business head, Raychem RPG

'Understanding organizational requirements, envisaging apt solutions, fostering client partnerships and ensuring project delivery are all critical success factors from a client's perspective. The knowledge required for this is vast, and Sandeep Krishnan has shared it in an in-depth way with an interesting storyline. An absorbing read!'—Sabu Thomas, chief people office, Allstate India

THE **MIND** OF A
CONSULTANT

LEVERAGING A CONSULTING
MINDSET FOR PROFESSIONAL SUCCESS

SANDEEP K. KRISHNAN

AUTHOR OF *THE MAKING OF A CEO*

PORTFOLIO
PENGUIN

An imprint of Penguin Random House

PORTFOLIO

USA | Canada | UK | Ireland | Australia
New Zealand | India | South Africa | China

Portfolio is part of the Penguin Random House group of companies
whose addresses can be found at global.penguinrandomhouse.com

Published by Penguin Random House India Pvt. Ltd
4th Floor, Capital Tower 1, MG Road,
Gurugram 122 002, Haryana, India

Penguin
Random House
India

First published in Portfolio by Penguin Random House India 2021

Copyright © Sandeep K. Krishnan 2021

All rights reserved

10 9 8 7 6 5 4 3 2 1

ISBN 9780670093946

Typeset in Sabon by Manipal Technologies Limited, Manipal

www.penguin.co.in

'Every year in consulting is like three years in the corporate world, because you have multiple clients, multiple issues—you grow so much'

—Indra Nooyi, former CEO, PepsiCo

Contents

Introduction

Exciting—that's the word I would use to describe the life of a management consultant. It's definitely a demanding profession—one that many aspire to, many participate in, many quit and only some thrive in. Demanding clients, exciting problems to solve, and a challenging work schedule— a consultant's life is never boring.

In my years spent consulting, I have observed many great consultants and reflected often on what I believe makes them stand out. I believe it's a unique combination of knowledge and a lot of personal qualities developed over time. You'll observe these reflections in many chapters of this book.

Samanta Thomas is a character wrought of my imagination. She is the epitome of a consultant—a woman of substance, who learns how to handle both her tribulations and successes with equal ease. This is her journey, and the journey of many consultants who chose to tread this path of excellence in the consulting field.

This book is not just for the Samanta Thomas's of the professional world, though. The insights and lessons she learns on her journey of professional growth are universal. These can help any professional experience a fruitful career. Current and aspiring consultants will find it a reflection of the workings of their own firms, and how it provides a bird's-eye view of their work ecosystems. This book will provide other business professionals with key skills that will help them excel in their respective fields. As you read this book, I encourage you to reflect on your strengths and areas of opportunity. Your two options are to work on yourself and become the best you can be, or look back on your failures and cry over spilt milk. As Robert T. Kiyosaki, author of *Rich Dad Poor Dad*,[1] said, 'Winners are not afraid of losing. But losers are. Failure is part of the process of success. People who avoid failure also avoid success.'

Each one of us, no matter how successful we are, have experienced failures in our career. Even the best of us still have to face challenges and overcome the roadblocks keeping us from success. Samanta takes us through this journey of experiencing failure and then bouncing back. It's not an easy process, and many go off-track along the way. The process may require us to gain a deeper understanding of ourselves as professionals and reinvent ourselves to keep growing. The goal of this book is to help clarify our objectives and refocus for greater success.

I present some of the critical skills needed to develop a great consulting mind. While the book covers serious career and consulting skills, which tend to be technical in nature, I opted to use a storytelling style as my framework to convey my concepts and teachings. Samanta's journey

---

[1]   Robert T. Kiyosaki, *Rich Dad Poor Dad: What the Rich Teach Their Kids about Money That the Poor and Middle Class Do Not!*, Ingram Publisher Services, 2018.

1 – provid support
on a firm
bias from

isn't far from the reality many in management consulting face every day. I have used creative licence to make the story interesting for you, the reader, but have done my best to stay as close to real life as possible and provide you with insight into the business and consulting world. Samanta's growth journey is undergirded with multiple expert opinions that will give you deeper insights into the skills discussed.

Some of the core skills I cover, such as critical thinking, analytical skills, communication/presentation skills and problem-solving, are foundational to any professional. A consultant tends to use them to a higher degree as a result of facing various client situations as part of the job. A section of the book is dedicated to outlining various tools and frameworks a consultant has at his/her disposal. I believe financial analysis and the ability to understand a business from the finance side is helpful in gaining a broader perspective of the company. Studying finance in depth requires effort and practice, but the resulting insight can be worth it. I cover some essential thoughts on financial literacy and its use to a professional in several areas of the book.

Many of the skills required for one to distinguish oneself in the consulting field are applicable to many other professionals as well. Skills such as change management, networking and selling skills, leadership and influence, and facilitation help a professional be identified as a key asset of the organization.

More advanced leadership and business-development skills are discussed in the chapter 'Standing on the Crest'. This chapter also covers the aspect of a partner in a consulting firm operating more like an entrepreneur.

The book explores many scenarios and case studies that a consultant would face. The case studies and lessons that can be learnt from them are as close as possible to reality. I encourage you to reflect on the situations presented and develop your own answers to them. I believe the book will help you in this reflection process.

1

At the Crossroads

Samanta Thomas rose from her chair as the meeting ended. Her team followed suit. The rest of the chairs were occupied by the board of directors and the top team of a large financial services firm—their client in this project. Samanta folded her arms and took a deep breath. The meeting had been stormy, to say the least—the epilogue to an organization transformation project she had been leading. The project involved a lot of strategic changes and aimed at preparing the organization for the future. In the three years that she had taken over as the director of consulting for the banking and financial industry practice at Pinnacle, she had never been in a situation like this. Nearly all of her recommendations had been shot down by the client after the first hadn't been received well. An avalanche, as they'd say in the firm. The tension had become so thick by the end of the meeting that two of the principal consultants and a junior analyst hadn't even been able to look at her.

Ram, the director of strategy for the financial services firm, beckoned to her. She and her team followed him into the guest room, the rest of her team crowding in behind her. She took a seat and leaned back in the chair. The meeting could have gone a whole lot better. She was grateful that Ram had been there, though. A tenured employee with the financial services firm, he had been an amazing partner throughout the whole assignment. He had a lot at stake in this presentation too. His board had pinned their hopes on this project, and the organization had invested more than $2 million in this assignment.

Samanta let out the breath she didn't know she was holding. She and her team had done their best. They'd done extensive research, picked the brains of key stakeholders and then presented their recommendations—after doing multiple rounds of iterations with Ram. She'd entered the meeting with such confidence. She had thought it would be a breeze to pass the recommendations with the top management and get things moving. But, instead, there was an avalanche!

Samanta was lost in her thoughts. She replayed the meeting over and over in her mind. Finally, she straightened up in her chair and looked around. She could sense the uneasiness in the guest room as her colleagues shifted in their seats or muttered to one another as they waited to hear what the client decided. The tension in the room was growing worse. Time to do something about it.

'That was pretty rough. An avalanche is never fun. Anyone has any feedback?'

John, the most senior member of the team, spoke. 'You did great in there, Sammy. You handled the pushback graciously. Nobody else would have handled it better than you.' He sighed and rubbed the back of his neck. 'I'm just worried we might have gotten the recommendation wrong.'

Gita, an analyst and the youngest member of the team, chimed in. 'You did great though, Sammy. Even during the most difficult moments, you were the most composed.'

Samanta nodded her thanks. They had done everything they could. Now all they could do was wait and see what the client would decide.

* * *

It had been ten years since Samanta joined Pinnacle. She had decided to take the plunge into a management career after graduating from a top engineering institute in electronics and telecommunication as a rank holder. She had applied to the number-one-ranked management institute in the country and was admitted after clearing what was considered one of the toughest admission tests then.

Her academic excellence continued into her MBA days. She always strove to do her best and enjoyed the competitive environment of the institute and the way it helped motivate her to higher levels of achievement. During her time there, she received the director's medal for academic and all-round performance (one of only a few to do so). She was the female representative at the student affairs council and the secretary of the management consulting club. She was also a nationally recognized fencer, representing her country in the game.

After the first year of her MBA, Samanta did her internship at Pinnacle. After only a short time there, she became the partners' top choice for a job offer. One of the partners wrote in his recommendation, 'Every couple of years, we get a bright spark like Samanta. Someone who works hard and is passionate about learning. In the two months she has spent working with us, she has contributed as much as if she had spent an entire year here. If Samanta were to be picked up by the competition, it would be a huge loss for us.'

Most students tended to slack off in their academics after hearing of a job offer. They spent more time enjoying life on campus, knowing their future was secure. For Samanta, though, it was the opposite. Success increased her determination to further her excellence. She spent her spare time doing pro-bono projects for companies near the campus and took extra credit courses that would help her in her consulting career. She had no time left for any other activity, but it was a sacrifice she was willing to make. She received the director's medal at her MBA convocation. She would look back on that day as one of the proudest of her life.

While she aced academics, her first year at Pinnacle was far from easy. There were now more variables than just her personal performance. The expectations of the clients, project managers, her peers and other seniors were suddenly crucial. If the management institute trained the cream of the country, Pinnacle trained the cream of the cream from similar institutes around the globe. Samanta would have given many of her new colleagues a ten out of ten in the areas that now mattered so much to her—academic performance, communication skills and a zeal for excellence.

Her first two weeks in the firm started with instructional talks by senior partners that ranged from client case studies and best work practices to what it took to be successful as a consultant. Three principles that stuck in her mind were:

1. Think and deliver beyond.
2. Deliver client success.
3. Build and leverage your network.

There was an additional point that one of the partners spoke about: 'Be yourself.' She emphasized that each person was unique, even though everyone in the firm shared common methodologies, work processes and values. This was the

X-factor that helped a team member stand out and have a better chance at being a successful partner in the firm. At the time, becoming a partner had sounded like conquering the summit of Mount Everest before even taking the first step towards it.

Nine years later, Samanta was an incredibly successful director, in line to be promoted to partner. The coveted position was within reach, just one ladder rung away.

The week of the promotion, she was called into the office. She listened, her heart in her throat, as she was asked to wait for some more time to be promoted. The recommendation was that she work on cultivating her independent identity in the industry circles.

Samanta was disappointed. She had brought in high revenue for the firm, her team loved her and she enjoyed great relationships with most of her clients. On top of all this, she had sacrificed her personal life for the firm. She worked through weekends, travelled extensively for business and spent personal time to help clients succeed. She had often been held up as the role model for aspiring consultants. They were told that if they wanted to succeed, they should follow Samanta's example. And this was the firm that was now asking her to wait and show progress of improvement before they could promote her. What made it even harder was watching her peers and batch mates celebrate their promotions to partner. They would be earning several times more than her in a few more years. And more than that, they were now part of an elite club and held a title every consultant dreamt of—partner. But the worst part was that she didn't know what had gone wrong.

She met her career guide and mentor, a senior partner, a week after the decision. He laid out the reasoning behind the upper management's decision. 'You're still not natural in your client engagement, Sammy,' he said, leaning forward in his chair.

'At times, it seems like you just follow a formula when talking to clients. Your recommendations seem formulaic too. Not every client needs a cookie cut-out approach—and that can easily lead to failure. You have to bring a natural sensing to the table.'

Samanta walked out of the meeting more than a little dejected. After years of working with multiple clients, deep research on industry sectors and an amazing ability to bring in more business, she had heard that she was failing due to a lack of something that couldn't even be quantified. She had rejected multiple offers from the competition and other industry colleagues, and they had offered her much better salaries and positions than what she had currently. CEOs had called her, asking her to join their top teams. And now she was being stonewalled in her career advancement by her company through flimsy feedback. It was ironic.

The Mentor

Samanta thought about that meeting for weeks, getting more and more depressed every time she did. How could she fix something if she didn't know what her shortcomings were?

She decided to set up a meeting with her informal mentor, Ivan Raphael. Ivan was the managing director of a well-known global consulting firm. He served on the board of various corporations and was highly respected in the industry. Samanta had met Ivan at one of the board presentations she had done several years ago. Ivan had been an adviser for the board to help the company finalize its mergers and acquisition strategy for growth. Samanta had done a thorough analysis on why acquisition was its best option for growth. During the presentation, she had stressed the need for geographic and innovative product introduction. Ivan had asked her only one question during the presentation: 'Have you read the promoters' mindset for acquisition? What are their fears related to pursuing an acquisition strategy?' Samanta had given the usual responses for why the promoters would benefit from the strategy, but she didn't really have a clue about whether the strategy would fly with them.

Ivan had made it a point to seek her out after the presentation. He had emphasized the importance of considering the mindset of the founder promoters when presenting a recommendation. Considerations such as how much they valued the culture they had built, the importance of family governance and how they might not be comfortable dealing with too much change management. Samanta had never valued these areas before. She had thought of herself as a change agent. Her role was to encourage the leadership team to take a leap in a new direction. She hadn't felt like it was her job to reinforce the promoters' beliefs. However, Ivan's guidance in that particular case had helped her get more buy-in from the promoters and allowed her to draft a change agenda with them.

They had stayed in touch ever since. Ivan often gave her advice that helped her navigate tough client situations. He also gave her access to his network, which helped her build her own group of consulting clients.

As they sat down for their meeting, Samanta could tell Ivan was amused. She knew he had seen many high-performing consultants in his career who shared the same concerns she did. She was grateful that they shared a solid relationship that allowed him to shoot straight with her.

'Sammy, what you're going through isn't new,' he said, a smile in his eyes. 'As you probably know, I've had many consultants come through who struggled with the same issues. But I think you're even more equipped to deal with them than the others.' He held up his hand and began to count off on his fingers. 'You're committed to the profession. You're a hard worker. You understand business needs. You know how to build and support a team. And, the best thing,' he said, wiggling the last finger, 'is that you're willing to learn. You have a unique ability to learn from different sources— be it from industry leaders, experts in various fields, through self-study or from your own team members. Because of that, you're deeply knowledgeable in any area related to the industry.'

He leaned back in his chair. 'Listen, I know this is a hard time for you. And I'm not sure that Pinnacle made the right decision in not promoting you.' He smiled. 'I think I would have promoted you without a second thought. But if there are concerns they brought up, let's do what we can to address them.'

He reached into a desk drawer and brought out a piece of paper. He handed it to Samanta. There were two columns running down the length of the sheet. The left-hand column had 'Competence' typed on top and the right-hand column 'Self-Rating'. He gestured at the paper. 'What would you say are the capabilities of a successful partner? And how would you rate yourself on each?'

She took a deep breath and started to write.

Competence	Self-Rating
Analytical thinking	Excellent
Industry/practice knowledge	Excellent
Problem-solving skills	Excellent
Delivery excellence	Excellent
Team management	Good
Client management	Excellent
Business development	Good

It was only a few minutes before she handed the paper back to him. He looked it over and nodded. 'Knowing you, I'd say these ratings are pretty accurate.' A smile tugged on the corners of his mouth. 'Though I think you're being a bit conservative on your team-management-skills rating.' She couldn't help smiling back.

He tapped the paper with his index finger and frowned. 'But I will say I'm not sure you fully understand what the real skills required to be a partner are.'

He laced his fingers together and looked at her. 'I want you to ask yourself these three questions:

1. When was the last time you brought a fundamentally new idea for the firm to be more competitive?
2. Are you recognized as an expert outside the firm? Are you an invited speaker for even a few well-known events in your industry? Do you have a personal brand?
3. Can you spot business opportunities beyond what others can see?'

He sat back down. 'You consider these questions and see if it makes a difference in how you perform.'

And she did.

* * *

Samanta could see the board members coming out of the meeting room. They'd come to a decision. Ram was with them, and seemed to be having a serious discussion with one of them. Samanta wished she could hear what they were saying. Ram glanced her way and signalled to her that he would be with her soon. He said a few final words to the board member, shook his hand and headed her way.

Ram looked visibly relieved. 'The board was excited about the second option you presented—Plan B—and they'd like to explore it further.'

She nodded. It was good and bad news. It meant that 95 per cent of the work and research she and her team had put into the project about the industry as a whole, the competition and the firm itself was now irrelevant. But the good news was that the board wanted to explore Plan B, a new growth strategy she had suggested that revolved around using digital transformation as the approach to go to market. The board also wanted to explore her idea for a new business line.

It was a kind of sixth sense that told her to think out of the box when providing this recommendation. The old Samanta would have never thrown a solution out there without in-depth research and hard numbers to back it up.

Still, could she really be sure that she had done the right thing? How was she to know if the client was making the right decision based on her recommendation? Maybe it was the decade of experience and her depth of understanding for the industry that had helped her in just a short time to blend the aspiration of the client, the industry trends and the new models of doing business that had been opened up by digital transformation. It was definitely a huge leap from what she had been doing throughout most of her consulting life. She smiled. Maybe this was the new Samanta.

2

The Beginning

It had been just three months that Samanta had started going to the management institute, and she was doing well. This was due in part to her senior, Jacob.

Jacob was one of the most popular guys at the institute. An all-rounder, by most standards—exceptional in studies, an avid tennis player and, most importantly, highly respected. Samanta saw him as a role model. He had been given offers from all the major consulting firms. They were literally selling him internship opportunities. Among all those offers, Jacob had chosen to intern with Pinnacle.

Jacob had become an informal adviser to Sammy. She could tell that he respected her focus and, above all, her keen intellect, which he could relate to.

One day, while they were chatting, Jacob challenged her to take her skills to the next level.

'Sammy, you need to get your case interview right. With your credentials, they should be thinking about why *not* to hire you.'

Samanta nodded. She knew how important her case interview was. Preparing for it boiled down to practical application of the concepts and problem-solving techniques learnt during the first few months at management school. But doing it well was the challenge.

Jacob shifted in his chair and stared into space.

'There are four critical aspects of clearing the case interview that will go a long way in helping you get selected to a top-tier consulting firm.' She leaned closer as he held up a finger.

'First, be smart and engaging. Second,' he said as he raised the second finger, 'think in an integrated manner. Third, show eagerness and learnability. And, finally, show them you are one of them.'

Samanta repeated the points in her head:

1. Be smart and engaging.
2. Think in an integrated manner.
3. Show eagerness and learnability.
4. Show them you are one of them.

She knew he was right. She had already seen the need for exactly those four things as she had started preparing for her case interview.

At Pinnacle, the first part of the selection centred on a brief problem-solving test. This involved analysing short cases and providing solutions. While Samanta had spent more than three months in the company learning how to handle different problems, the case interpretation and recommendation they would be looking for would have to be more comprehensive and not just parroting answers she had learnt. She had spent more than enough time pondering various case-based interview formats and frameworks, but now she would have to prove that she understood the problems at the foundational level and could create her own solutions based on her thorough knowledge of the key principles behind the frameworks.

One advice Jacob had given her about this had stuck. 'The problem-solving test isn't to see how many frameworks you know, but how well you can apply them. It's okay if you don't use any of them. But come up with a solution that would make it interesting to the decision maker in the case study—which is usually the CEO—and you're well on your way to making an effective recommendation. You have to put yourself in the CEO's shoes.'

Preparation wasn't easy. There were hours of case videos to watch that covered different elements of solving a case. There were interview samples from Pinnacle and their top competitors to analyse. It took hours of focused effort to go through the breadth of knowledge available on solving case problems. Samanta found that there were interesting frameworks that could be used to solve business problems. She also turned to the bible of case-based problem-solving—*Case in Point*[1] by Marc Cosentino.

Three elements were critical there:

1. Understanding and assimilating the frameworks into one's problem-solving. However, one is the master of the framework and not the other way round. Force-fitting a solution to a framework may not yield the best solution.
2. Having a blend of a quantitative and qualitative mind. It is important to speak numbers—even approximations. The blend of understanding the situation completely might require thinking with numbers, and also a qualitative appreciation. Good consultants constructed the story with an effective blend of numbers and their own ideas/assumptions.

---

[1] Marc P. Cosentino, *Case in Point: Complete Case Interview Preparation*, Zaccheus Entertainment, 2018.

3. Working in the context of a team. The whole is greater than the sum of its parts.

Interview with Marc Cosentino, author of *Case in Point*

Cosentino, one of the world's foremost authorities on case-interviewing, has thirty years of experience with case questions. He has written well over a hundred cases, while coaching, preparing and training more than 1,50,000 students and alumni. He has written four books involving cases and consulting.

1. A case reflects a real business situation. Is there a right approach to solving a case problem?

    For a case analysis or a case interview, the steps are to scope the problem first, listen and clarify. This is to really understand the information provided and the problem that is described in the case. The second step is to break down the problem and identify business drivers and issues. The third step is to analyse the problem. This involves interpreting the data in detail. The fourth step is to come up with plausible solutions and communicate those ideas to the client, so they buy into your solutions.

    If there is a case-based interview, it would involve the process described below:

    -   Summarizing the questions that are asked in the case.
    -   Verifying the objectives of the case.
    -   Enquiring if there are any sub-objectives.

- Asking clarifying questions, say, on industry terminologies you are not aware of.
- Laying out the structure or the framework for analysis, making sure that your structure is MECE (mutually exclusive collectively exhausted—meaning there should be no overlap in your structure).
- Stating an initial hypothesis.

In case interviews, coming up with a hypothesis is an important element to understanding the consulting mindset of a candidate.

2. What are some of the skills you think make for a good consultant?

In my experience, some of the skills that set apart a great consultant from an average one are:
- Critical thinking
- Structure of thought
- Communication skills, including persuasion skills
- Analytical thinking, including quantitative ability
- Creative or innovative thinking

Critical thinking, structure of thought and analytical thinking are fundamentals. Without this, one cannot analyse a case or come up with plausible solutions. Communication skills are critical for client management and even collaborating in a consulting organization. It is persuasive communication that helps a client buy into your ideas and thoughts.

Another important element of communication is clarity. In a consulting interview, if a candidate speaks without logic or is not able to connect the dots, there is a chance that he or she is 'talking before thinking'. This can be perilous in a consulting environment.

In most of the consulting interviews, a candidate who has innovative or creative solutions often has an edge over the others. In a short time, if one can be calm and think on their feet, it is a definite advantage in a consulting environment.

3. How important are theories and frameworks for a consultant?

It's about structure of thought, about what goes through the interviewee's mind when they hear a problem. While it is important to have a structure in terms of solution, often it is not desirable to force-fit a framework. Each framework needs to be handcrafted for the case. The important element that I have seen that firms look for in consultants is an ability to deeply understand the client first. But how does the client define success? Particularly when entering a new market case, you need a good understanding of the client before you look at the market, so you can analyse the new market from the client's point of view. In a profit-and-loss case, a good clarifying question would be, 'Are our competitors' profits down as well?' That allows the interviewee to determine whether this is the client's problem or an industry-wide issue.

4. What is the analysis on the case-interviewing process of firms such as McKinsey, Bain and BCG?

   At McKinsey, the objectives are clearly stated and expectations from the candidate are more structured. It is called an interviewer-led case. However, in case of a Bain or a BCG interview, the context or case situation is provided, and it is up to the candidate to deduce the problem, and come up with the hypothesis and the solution. This requires deeper understanding and more critical thinking on the candidate's part. This is known as an interviewee-led case.

5. What are your recommendations for an aspirant to prepare for a case interview with major firms?

   Practice is an important element of preparation for case interviews. I would recommend at least sixty hours. Ideally, if one is able to analyse about thirty cases, it would help build the candidate's skills. However, it is important to go deeper and, sometimes, more insights are uncovered if the candidate reads the same case thrice. Discussion and group preparation also help, since multiple insights are derived from the group members. I would also recommend recording the discussion and seeing how confidently one is presenting. Keeping a journal to track one's progress also helps.

6. Is case analysis a skill for any professional career?

Case analysis and preparation for a case interview instil skills in a candidate such as breaking down a problem, identifying the drivers of a problem/ identifying the issues and communicating with impact. The solution mindset also builds up. Overall, critical thinking is developed in the process. These skills are useful throughout one's career, whether in consulting or any other profession.

Samanta started working with a group of like-minded students. Working with the group helped her understand that a situation could be viewed from multiple angles. She realized what was meant by 'the whole is greater than the sum of its parts'. The group and their ability to dissect the details of the case helped her realize the potential of each of the problems and what to expect in the interview.

She remembered a discussion she and Jacob had once had. Jacob had asked some very interesting questions that he said would be asked in the personal interview with Pinnacle as well as other consulting firms. One of the questions was, 'If you get a chance to meet the chairman of a large business conglomerate in an elevator, how would you introduce yourself?' It was a fancy way of making someone build an 'elevator pitch'. Samanta did her best to answer the question in the most interesting way she could think of. She spoke about her background, where she had studied and how much she admired the chairman. Jacob told her she had done well but that she might only just get a nod from the chairman.

What is an elevator pitch?

An elevator pitch is a short, impactful speech that one uses to make the other person interested in them or the organization one represents. A good elevator pitch can get the audience interested in one's idea, one's organization or one as a professional. A good elevator pitch is to be made in the amount of time one has with someone in an elevator—usually less than thirty to forty seconds.

Three tips for creating a great elevator pitch:

- Identify your goal for the conversation.
- Show confidence and have an open body language.
- Speak about your USP—what differentiates you from the competition that will interest your audience.

Jacob shared many other potential questions that could be asked at the interview:

Where do you see your career in ten years' time?

Tell us something you do in your free time.

If you had a month of vacation, what would you do?

How would you feel if you had to take twenty flights and stay fifteen days in a hotel in a single month?

How would your best friend describe you?

Jacob also said that the questions the interviewers asked usually went beyond just getting to know the interviewee and dove into how they had performed in the past. Questions such as:

Tell us about a failure you had and how you dealt with it.

Give an example of how you planned something and how you involved others.

Give an example of how you persuaded a group to do something they really weren't interested in.

Give an example of a change you brought in yourself in the past few years.

'Remember,' Jacob told her. 'The firm is looking to hire people who have a high chance of being successful in a consulting career, are analytical, with a penchant for problem-solving, and are articulate and engaging.'

The day finally came when the selection process started. There were two senior consultants and a senior partner who had individual discussions with Samanta. As she talked to them, she couldn't help but realize how much Jacob's support was helping. One of the interviewers asked her what one of the greatest accomplishments in her life was up to that point. She suppressed a smile. This was playing to her advantage. She told him about winning the national championship in fencing. The interviewer was curious. He asked more about fencing, how she had managed to be so proficient in the sport and, above all, what it took to be a great fencer. This time she really did smile. She loved talking about her fencing journey. Fencing was her forte. And now, all those years of practice and dedication were coming to her rescue in this critical juncture of her life.

'Fencing is about agility, focus and speed. You need to have a strong combination of those three to ace the game. You have to anticipate and plan infractions of seconds. Your body and mind must be in top condition. And the whole spirit of the sport is "play to win".'

In the next round of the process, during her meeting with the senior partner, the senior consultant introduced Samanta as 'the fencing champion'. It boosted her confidence and positioned her as a successful candidate right at the start. Once in her comfort zone, the discussions came naturally to her. It was as if she were having a wonderful discussion with people she knew very well and, as a result, she built excellent connections during the interviews.

Another area that piqued the interest of the interviewers was her keen interest in the stock market. She had a portfolio of close to $25,000 and had made an average return of 38 per cent every year for the past several years. The interviewers asked her about her interest in the share market and she explained how the shares helped her study the companies and their growth plans in depth. Investor presentations done by some of the firms also helped her understand things such as industry dynamics, key challenges of the sector and how the company was planning to tackle those challenges.

The senior partner asked about some of the companies she actively followed in the stock market and was particularly interested in one of the companies she mentioned. He asked her why the stock for the company was underperforming, even though the order books and growth prospects for the company were good. Samanta shared some of her views on the performance of the stocks and explained that the company was more present- than future-focused. Because of this, the stock market didn't see value in the company, or a strategy that would give multifold returns in future. The company hadn't invested in technology or new processes and solutions, so it was quite possible that their competitors would scale more than the company would in future, and get better results. The senior partner seemed pleased with Samanta's analysis.

'This kind of insight from an MBA student is rare,' he said, nodding in approval. 'I'm sure the CFO or the CEO of the company would like to hear your thoughts.'

Later in her career, following the stock market and actively researching the companies had helped quite a bit in her consulting career. Promoters and CEOs would respect her views on why their stocks were performing or underperforming.

The Case Interviews

While the personal interviews went well, the most important part was the problem-solving/case interviews. Samanta had been preparing thoroughly by studying multiple case studies on the websites of consulting companies, reading case-preparation material and books that were available on campus, and absorbing and applying the suggestions she had received from Jacob. She had also benefited from studying some of the important frameworks that were available to students to help them prepare, including those by Victor Cheng—a former consultant and an expert in preparing for consulting careers.

The problem-solving interviews were interesting. One of the problems they gave her was whether a large conglomerate should break into e-commerce with their retail venture, which included electronics, FMCG and fashion. Solving the problem was a matter of assessing the market attractiveness. Samanta had a structured approach whenever she looked at the market attractiveness. She started with the industry attractiveness using Porter's Five Forces analysis. She considered the existing competition in the space, how government policies were influencing the industry, customer/buyer preferences and how effective it would be to move from a large retail format to the e-commerce model from a supplier's perspective.

Through the analysis, she concluded that the space was moderately attractive, provided the conglomerate was ready to invest in the long term and willing to work on attractive pricing and marketing. Her recommendation was to go ahead with the plan, just so long as the conglomerate had the bandwidth to invest in the long term and the e-commerce venture supported the long-term growth prospects of the company as a whole.

The senior partner grilled Samanta on her recommendations. He pointed out the strengths of the competition and how prominent their customer brands already were. He explained how difficult it would be for a new player to make a dent in the market. On top of that, he pointed out that Samanta hadn't mentioned the growth of the e-commerce market and the enablers of the same.

Samanta responded evenly and pointed out her own analysis even more strongly, along with mentioning additional assessments she could provide, if necessary. She stood by her recommendation and outlined the steps the client should take to implement the e-commerce initiative over the next three years. The senior partner tried to question her logic at every juncture but Samanta stood firm but gracious. She tried to clearly convey to the partner that she was capable of approaching solutions in a logical way and back up her recommendations with analysis and hard data every time due to her extensive research. She also wanted to show that she could still believe strongly in her solution without coming across as adamant.

She remembered one of the videos she had watched on consulting that had stated, 'A good consultant is like a good doctor. She does a thorough diagnosis, looks for more data if required and makes sure the prescription is in the best interest of the patient. It is important that the doctor weigh the risks of their recommended option and convey their thoughts with conviction.'

Another case problem she was presented with was related to the airline industry. She was asked about an airline that was making a profit during the previous quarter until it reported a loss in the current quarter. The premise was that she had been hired to understand the detailed reasons behind why the loss had occurred and then come up with a plan to help the airline remain profitable in future. She had to admit that this was a great scenario for understanding how a consultant thought and approached a situation.

Samanta had two hypotheses about why the losses were occurring in the current quarter. One was that the loss was due to a dip in revenues and the other was that the losses were due to an increase in costs. It could also be a combination of both. She then mapped out the potential reasons for both the hypotheses.

Revenue Impact	Cost Impact
Lower price per seat	Fuel price
Discounts	New sectors
Less occupancy	One-time costs
Flight disruptions	HR/labour cost increase
	Aircraft costs—leasing, maintenance, insurance, etc.

Samanta analysed each issue and came up with a list of possibilities. It could have been an increase in the fuel prices, seasonal occupancy issues, discounting of fares due to competition and/or introduction of new sectors that increased costs but might give returns over the next few quarters or a possible one-time cost incurrence in that quarter. As she dug deeper, she asked for more data that helped her understand the situation better. While fuel prices had been stable, the airline had introduced new sectors and more aircraft. This would have also led to discounting of fares to attract initial traffic. The possible cause of the dip in the profit might have been due to multiple factors related to the introduction of new aircraft and sectors.

The senior partner was happy with her conclusion and mentioned that he thought she was able to do a bit of 'systems' thinking as well as standard problem-solving. She had the ability to see the interrelationship of various factors that could influence a situation, instead of just isolating the root cause.

While most of the interviews went well, not everything was smooth-sailing. One senior consultant wasn't very impressed with Samanta. He said that while she came across as structured in her approach, her ability to think on her feet could be improved. The questions the senior consultant asked were straightforward but not easy to respond to. Questions such as:

How many gas stations do you think there are in a particular state?

How many mobile-phone users are there in the country between the ages of eighteen and twenty-five?

What percentage of airline passengers do you think travel for business?

She thought these questions were strange and impossible to answer accurately without a proper research document. She realized that the consultant was trying to understand how she would address challenging problems such as these. While she was struggling to come up with answers, he decided to focus on the last question—about the percentage of business travellers in a typical flight.

Samanta asked a few clarifying questions that would help her come up with a good answer. 'Can I look at the typical business sectors separately? For example, the traffic to business cities such as New York, London or Mumbai would be having a very different percentage than sectors between tier-2 towns or cities,' she said. The senior consultant responded in the affirmative. 'Let us look at those sectors separately. Should I also look at budget versus full service?' The consultant nodded. Sammy knew that these factors could make a considerable difference in the percentages.

She took a deep breath and answered as confidently as she could. She concluded that if it were during a morning or an evening flight, between busy business sectors, approximately 50 to 60 per cent would be business travellers. She stated that a flight in the afternoon or at an odd hour would comprise around 20 per cent business travellers. That being the case, on average, approximately 30–40 per cent would be travelling for business, and 60–70 per cent for personal purpose. She also mentioned that this percentage could be 5–10 per cent higher if they took only full-service airlines. The consultant nodded, and told her that her estimates were not far away from the actual statistics.

The consultant asked another question to Samanta. 'What is the relevance of this data?' It made Samanta think again. 'Business travel must be more lucrative for the airlines. Many of them would travel business-class or might be booking last-minute with higher fares compared to non-business passengers? It must be a very important factor that will impact the airline profitability.' The senior consultant was busy noting down her answers.

Samanta wasn't sure if she would get the final offer from the firm. On the same day, she had two more interviews with other firms. One of them was a coveted investment banking firm, which was offering her almost three times the internship stipend of any other firm and the chance to work on Wall Street. It was definitely an attractive offer that many of her friends could only dream of.

By the end of the two days of interviews, Samanta had three offers in hand. Two were from consulting firms, including Pinnacle, and another from the investment bank. She went to talk to Jacob, who was very happy for her. He said that the only question she had to answer now was, 'Why consulting?'[2]

---

[2] Refer to Appendix 1 on 'Campus Experience—Making It to Consulting' for the real-life experiences of three students on getting selected to top consulting firms.

3

The Intern

'Is the presentation ready?' Hamid was unapologetic in his question.

It was 2 a.m. Samanta had been working for more than eighteen hours straight on the presentation for the client leadership team that was to be presented the next day. She was expected to be part of the presenting team alongside Hamid, the project manager and partner who owned the account. Hamid was six years her senior and from the same institute she was attending. He was highly respected by his colleagues and the project team members looked to him for guidance.

She thought back over the past few weeks, remembering the first day she had arrived at Pinnacle for her internship. It was like a dream come true. Her first official day as an intern at Pinnacle. She, along with thirty-five fellow interns from some of the best management institutes in the world, had been participating in the internship orientation. Two of the senior partners and a few engagement managers who could make it were part of the two-day programme.

While partners spoke about the culture and the attributes of great consultants, the engagement managers were more operational. They spoke about the tools and the support that were available to interns. They shared Pinnacle's knowledge base, along with templates for PPTs and Excel sheets, which were life-savers for the interns when they started out.

At the end of the second day, the interns were provided with laptops and their project assignments. Samanta was assigned to a large organization-transformation project in the retail industry. The organization was exploring strategies to enhance growth and increase efficiency amid changing industry dynamics. Her project manager for the assignment was Hamid. At the time, Hamid was participating in more than half a dozen similar assignments worldwide. He was always up to date on the latest happenings in the industry and often considered an expert in the field.

The first time Samanta and Raghav, a fellow intern, met Hamid to work on the project, he came across as passionate and knowledgeable. It was obvious that he was an accomplished consultant.

'I want you guys to challenge me,' he told them. 'It's important that you get a head start and not waste time doing things that don't matter to this project.'

He gave them presentations and materials to read, a brief on the client requirements and the names of some resources in the firm that he thought could be helpful.

'Get ready to fly out tomorrow to meet the client,' he said. 'We're having meetings with some of the key management team members before doing a few store visits to understand their set-up. You need to be up to speed on everything that we know about the client by then.'

One thing Samanta learnt from Day One was that consulting constantly needed one to learn and travel. That was the best part about being at Pinnacle. It treated its team members as star talent, and believed that its people could figure out a way to deliver on even the toughest assignments.

Samanta and Raghav spent their time leading up to their trip reading more on the retail industry in general and the company in particular. Pinnacle had some wonderful case studies and industry knowledge available that they found helpful. There were different terminology and business metrics that Samanta and Raghav had never encountered before, but Hamid encouraged them to learn all of it, and learn it well.

'You don't want to be seen as novices. You should be able to ask and understand questions in areas that are relevant even to the CEO.'

The following day, Samanta, Raghav and Hamid started on their trip to see the client. Samanta had been told that she was lucky to be doing her first project with Hamid, so she took advantage of the uninterrupted cab drive to ask him questions. There was one in particular she couldn't help asking.

'How did you earn so much respect from your peers?'

Hamid raised his eyebrow at her, a smile on his face. Samanta shifted uncomfortably in her seat. She was probably the first intern to ever ask him that.

Hamid gave a short laugh at her discomfort before answering. 'How do you think, Sammy? And you too, Raghav.'

Samanta thought for a moment. There were several possible reasons, or, more likely, a combination of several of them.

Raghav chimed in first. 'Maybe hard work? Or domain knowledge?'

Samanta nodded. She had been thinking along the same lines. She added her own thoughts. 'I would think project-management expertise would have something to do with it. Is that part of the reason?'

Hamid nodded and smiled. 'All of those are correct, but there are three main rules I live by in this firm.' He held up his fingers as he counted them off.

'Rule 1: Strive for knowledge.

'Rule 2: Build your best coalition.

'Rule 3: Always be ahead of the client.

'Each of these is critical when working as a consultant.'

He shifted in his chair and began to explain further. 'Rule 1, striving for knowledge, is the essential, golden rule. In consulting, you can't survive without having deep understanding and knowledge. It can be knowledge about the industry you're working in, or about your specific project or full comprehension of the frameworks one uses and relies on. It's always important for you to be ahead of the curve. As for me, apart from what I learn while working on my projects, I spend at least three to four additional hours a week enhancing my knowledge. I've done everything from reading industry magazines, noting down important industry events and reviewing news articles to reading the latest research or books related to my work. And recently, I've expanded my sphere of learning by studying areas that could influence my industry field. For example, the clients are very interested in how technology is influencing their respective industries and what their competitors or other companies are doing to stay ahead of the curve. Attending some of the industry conferences has helped me be better prepared in such situations.

'Next, there's Rule 2: Build your best coalition. In my first year in the firm itself, I understood it was important to build a strong network and an ecosystem that would help me perform at my best and deliver on assignments. I split these ecosystems into two categories: the immediate and the long-term. The immediate ecosystem is the team and support, which helps me deliver the best outcome on the current project. My project sponsor, my team members, my peers, the research team and the client team are the key elements of the immediate coalition. The long-term ecosystem is the network I am building on a regular basis—the global network of consultants in the firm, the industry experts, the industry leaders, the industry bodies and the industry publications. I try to build at least two new business relationships every week and seek their advice or provide suggestions for them.

'About Rule 3—always be ahead of the client—engagement and client satisfaction are critical. My philosophy is to anticipate what the client will ask or expect. It always pays off for me and the firm to be ahead of the curve. But this requires having a deep sense of the requirements of the board and the top decision makers in the company. Sometimes I try to surprise them with ideas I don't think they've thought of before. The moment they see the value of bringing in Pinnacle and having me as the project manager, I believe every assignment becomes much easier to execute.

'All of these require the qualities you mentioned—hard work, domain knowledge and, of course, project management. I would add two more qualities that are essential—confidence and relationship-building. Confidence comes from a full knowledge of your subject, and the skill of expressing yourself and making your presence felt. Just make sure you have the knowledge and the expertise to back up what you say when you express yourself, or you'll end up looking like a fool. On the other hand, be sure to show confidence by expressing yourself when you genuinely have insight into the subject. Otherwise, the client won't see your value.'

It was great watching Hamid get more and more passionate as he explained the three rules he lived by that he considered his consulting secret sauce. What really struck Samanta was his interest in mentoring and sharing his wisdom with the interns—in this case, her and Raghav. After all, he wasn't much older than them. Five to six years, at the most. The real difference was that he came across as someone much older and more mature. Maybe that was what a consulting career did to a person. It made sense. Being a consultant opened the door to working with some of the sharpest minds in the industry and interacting with some of the biggest names in the business world.

* * *

Samanta took a sip from her coffee cup and sighed. Nothing beat a good espresso! Hamid was vocal about his choice of coffee as they sat in the business lounge. They had some time before they needed to board, so Hamid had led them there. It was a new experience for Samanta and Raghav, to be able to pass time in such an exclusive place. It was Pinnacle's policy to take care of its employees and the status of the firm at the same time, and this meant that team members often flew business class and stayed in the best five-star hotels.

Hamid exchanged pleasantries with some of their fellow travellers at the lounge. Samanta realized as she listened to their conversations that a few of them were former clients, and several were professional contacts. She smiled at the thought that this was probably part of him building his coalition team as per Rule 3.

Hamid became more serious when they started having breakfast in the lounge. He shared more about the client with them. Samanta and Raghav were all ears. Hamid mentioned that the client had hit a plateau in terms of growth. The promoters' earlier thoughts had been to establish a large retail chain in the country in five to six years and then exit fully or partially by selling to another firm that might be interested in making it grow further. However, regulation changes in the retail industry, an increase in losses due to rapid expansion and tough competition had led to them re-evaluating their strategy. Making an exit from the business wasn't looking as feasible anymore, given the situation. The promoters had brought in Pinnacle to make the business more attractive to potential investors and to help them improve efficiency so the losses could be contained.

Hamid went on to share information about the promoters and pointed out some of the key management team members.

'As you know, the promoters are from the family of a large conglomerate. It's a brother–sister team in their mid-thirties. They are Ivy League-educated and are currently being mentored by their father, who is the chairman of the conglomerate. The retail business has turned out to be an opportunity for the third generation of the family to prove itself.'

Hamid took a sip of water from his glass and continued. 'They have a CEO who was in senior management at an FMCG firm prior to joining their company. He makes most of the operational decisions, and the operating team reports directly to him. The promoters still play a key role, though, because they decide what strategic decisions to make. So it will be important for us to have the approval of the promoters as well as the CEO.'

Hamid went on to outline the roles of each member of the senior management team, as well as his impressions of them.

Name of member	Role	Characteristics
Alan	Promoter; managing director	Practical, business-like, inclusive in decision-making, analytical, data-driven and strict about timelines.
Ziva	Promoter; deputy managing director	Creative and loves to hear new and big ideas.
Nikhil	CEO	Serious, analytical, operation-driven, with a data-based approach.

It was insightful for Sammy that the personality and the characteristics of the business leaders could influence how they might look at inputs and decision-making. In the very functional approach that B-schools took in their teaching approach, they rarely taught the importance of these factors.

In the four days the team spent with the client, they met more than twenty key management team members. Samanta and Raghav learnt the art of asking questions during this time. It was amazing to watch how Hamid asked questions and steered the conversation so the client was the one talking most of the time. And he employed a combination of questions that required both quantitative and qualitative answers.

Samanta and Raghav were in charge of following up to make sure all the right data was available for analysis. The various meetings they participated in gave them a fuller sense of what exactly was happening with the client and in the company. It was interesting to think that within four days of gathering information, she and the team probably knew more about the client's strategy and operation methods than some of its own members.

The three weeks after returning from the trip were hectic. Samanta and Raghav gained a full appreciation for the depth of work Pinnacle put into consulting. Two senior consultants continued working on the project while Samanta and Raghav were entrusted with collecting data on the industry trends and practices that would help move the project forward. From there, two management graduates in the making were responsible for aligning those trends and best practices with the potential strategy of the client.

Samanta was determined to give her best to make the greatest impact she could for the client. The wealth of information available with Pinnacle helped her immensely in this area. Studying past client case studies and industry research papers was like digging for buried treasure. She was able to review data and analysis that allowed her to understand the current project more deeply.

She also found that her fellow colleagues at Pinnacle were incredibly helpful. She asked for support and insight on several aspects of the project in the knowledge portal, and within a few hours, received three responses from across the various office locations at Pinnacle. One especially helpful colleague was Anne Chen, a senior consultant from China who was working on the retail sector. Anne gave Samanta interesting insights, along with three case studies to review.

The first study was of a company that moved forward and built more stores despite their losses, and wound up creating a monopoly by killing the other players. The second study was of a company that became niche by creating a handful of stores that offered new and different products. The third and final study outlined a company that built an e-commerce platform and focused on only a few stores that enabled them to scale up without encountering space challenges. It was a time when e-commerce was just picking up. The faster connectivity and advancing technology were fuelling e-commerce growth in a big way. The American retail sector was ahead of the curve and handling the challenge of the e-commerce boom well. Most traditional players who had made large retail space investment were facing profitability challenges.

Samanta tried to keep it all straight as she absorbed the deluge of information. The available data related to the current project was overwhelming. This was when Sammy learnt the importance of knowing how to plan one's analysis when too much information was available. She and Raghav were having endless conversations on what information would be important to the project, but were getting nowhere until Hamid came to their rescue. He told them to sort the information into three buckets in the form of questions:

1. What insights can we provide that will help the client understand why their company is in its current situation?
2. Are there industry players who have gone through the same situation? If yes, what did they try and what were the outcomes?
3. Are there options we can learn from the industry that might be applicable to the client?

After looking it over, Samanta and Raghav realized they had data that would probably help with all three questions. Now it was just a matter of structuring the presentation the way Hamid had suggested.

One of the interesting aspects that Isha, the senior consultant in the project, had drilled into their heads was the use of the 'Pyramid Principle' in presentations. The Pyramid

Principle was based on an idea put forth by Barbara Minto in her book *The Pyramid Principle: Logic in Writing and Thinking*.[1]

It focused on three key aspects:

1. Start with the answer, or your recommendation.
2. Convey the main reasons the recommendation should be considered as a top option in moving forward.
3. Present the details and analysis that will support the recommendation and reasons.

The Pyramid Principle was key in helping Samanta connect their research to the overall client presentation. Hamid had already worked out the top recommendation they would be presenting to the client, and now Samanta and Raghav's job was to add the relevant analysis and data they had compiled to support the recommendation.

Hamid was not an easy customer to work with. Samanta and Raghav sent their initial set of slides containing their compiled research to Isha. While Isha was working on the presentation, Hamid grilled them on the research they had done, asking at least twenty questions. He was asking the questions as if Samanta and Raghav had themselves worked on the earlier projects.

He was especially interested in knowing what had happened to the companies after they had followed the recommendations by Pinnacle. Samanta shared that the example that most closely matched the recommendation they were going to present to the current client had not done well when Pinnacle had proposed it the first time.

---

[1]   Barbara Minto, *The Pyramid Principle: Logic in Writing and Thinking*, Pearson, 3/e2020.

The company had experienced further losses and had thrown a distress sale! Hamid rubbed his hands, glad they had found that example. The company had cut losses, shut down loss-making stores and focused on profit increase—and yet did not succeed.

'The strategy wasn't the issue,' Hamid explained to Samanta and Raghav. 'The real issue was poor management. Many of the key management team members jumped ship during the restructuring. They were afraid of losing their jobs. This had a direct effect on their customer service and overall operations.' Both Samanta and Raghav could tell that Hamid wanted them to understand the point that a strategy was as good as its execution and the change-management team responsible for making it happen. Pinnacle's suggestion was sound, but it wasn't executed well. That was why following through was so important, as was keeping employee morale high during times of change and uncertainty.

Samanta reflected on what Hamid had said. 'The effectiveness of a strategy often lies in how well it is executed.'

Another key learning point she came away with was that, often, as a consultant, one had to guard oneself from being blinded by one's functional silos. The real reasons behind success and failure could be tied in with factors that might not be accounted for traditionally.

Overall, the internship project was a great opportunity to learn about systems thinking—an understanding that a single recommendation one is suggesting can impact the whole business.

And now, here she was, after weeks of preparation and learning, adding the final touches to the presentation. It was after 3 a.m. Earlier, Hamid had asked her to review the deck that was to be presented to the client. She had gone slide by slide and suggested changes wherever needed. Hamid and

Isha had given the presentation a final look and had accepted most of her suggested changes.

'I think you missed this one,' Hamid said. 'The colour codes don't match. This one's supposed to be green, but it's amber.'

Samanta looked at where he indicated and raised her brows. How had Hamid found such a tiny mistake? The incorrect shade was one in a block of twenty-four colour-coded dots. It was another learning moment for her. She realized that the devil indeed was in the details.

The presentation with the client the next day went well. Samanta and Raghav were amazed by the professionalism that Hamid and Isha exhibited during the presentation. They were crisp in their communication and listened intently to the comments of the client.

Ziva, the deputy managing director, was keenly interested in the global examples that were shared. At one point, Hamid asked Samanta to explain one of them. She did her best to speak to the point, and connected the example to the logic Hamid was driving home.

Nikhil, the CEO, wanted data and numbers to support the logic, and Isha presented the data clearly and confidently. She also shared a clear action plan for the desired change, and it was clear that he appreciated the inclusion.

The evening after the presentation was a lot of fun! The team partied late into the night, celebrating their successful presentation.

As they were parting ways, Hamid turned to Samanta and Raghav. 'Did you guys have fun? Did you enjoy it?'

Both nodded. 'Yes, we did,' Samanta said. But if she was being honest with herself, she was talking more about the presentation than the party!

The internship was a great opportunity for Samanta. She was able to pitch in on a great project, work with inspiring colleagues, gain some incredible knowledge and, above all, do something that matched her interests.

4

The Consultant

The second year of the MBA went by quickly for Samanta. Two months before the campus recruitment season started, she received a call from Hamid.

'Sammy, we want you to be part of our team,' he said. 'I'm recommending you to be hired at Pinnacle. I've talked to the rest of the team, and even the partner is excited to have you on board.' He paused as he let the words sink in. 'What do you think? Are you interested?'

Samanta couldn't believe what she was hearing. Her heart was beating faster at the news. 'I'm very interested. Give me a few days to think about it?' she said.

'You got it,' said Hamid.

Samanta called Jacob right away and told him what had happened. Jacob chuckled on the other end of the line.

'So many people are trying to get hired by Pinnacle that the company doesn't bother asking candidates to join them. The fact that they singled you out to be part of their team means they must be mighty impressed by you.'

Samanta knew that the second year of the MBA programme was an excellent opportunity to build her knowledge and conceptual skills. She wanted to learn a varied set of subjects and build a notable general-managerial profile in each of them. She felt this would help her continue to strengthen her skills as a consultant. While some of her friends relaxed after getting placements in top organizations, Samanta looked forward to more learning opportunities.

In the second year, Samanta had also gone for an international exchange programme to a business school in Denmark. The school was considered one of the best in Europe. It had a unique programme that enabled the exchange student to work in an organization while on the programme. It was an enlightening experience for Samanta.

One of the first things that struck her while she was there was that the people worked far fewer hours than she was used to. They spent a maximum of six to seven hours a day in office. But productivity was still high, with no wasted hours. There was clarity on deliverables and no ambiguity in terms of work output. This was a huge lesson for Sammy—understanding how to have maximum productivity, irrespective of the number of hours worked. It was an insight she was sure would come in handy in her career.

While in Denmark, Samanta also spent three days in the Copenhagen Pinnacle office. As a former intern and current MBA student, she was welcomed warmly. She spent much of the time observing and interacting with the team there.

Something that stood out to her about the consultants was their fitness level. Even though they had quite a hectic schedule at the Copenhagen office, they managed to exercise and stay in shape, making sure they also focused on their health and well-being. One of the consultants she met pointed out, 'Our clients are more impressed by a "fit" consultant than an "unfit" one. You can't use your busy schedule as an excuse for poor health.'

Another aspect she found quite different from the home office was a sense of order and confidence that pervaded the place. There was less of the usual office hustle and chaos, and more of a feeling of quiet efficiency. The consultants always seemed to be in control in any given situation.

She also found the team very helpful and supportive of her questions. This was enhanced by the fact that there was a sense of equality throughout the company, without a strong emphasis on the traditional hierarchy she had become accustomed to.

Her time of studying and exposure to new ideas at the Copenhagen office was a cultural learning experience for her. What she observed was in line with the training she had received at her institute about the cultural differences between countries, based on the teachings of Greet Hofstede.[1] Based on the Hofstede model, we can understand the scores of the national cultural dimensions as given in the table below:

Cultural Dimension	Score (100)	Implication
Power distance	18	How the society looks at hierarchy. In low power-distance societies, hierarchies are generally overlooked and equality in power is considered important.

---

[1] https://www.hofstede-insights.com/country-comparison/denmark/

Cultural Dimension	Score (100)	Implication
Individualism vs collectivism	74	In societies that are high on individualization, 'I' is more relevant than 'we'.
Masculinity vs femininity	16	This dimension speaks about tough vs tender in terms of how its members deal with each other.
Uncertainty avoidance	23	This dimension reflects how much a society is comfortable with ambiguity and uncertainty.
Long-term vs short-term orientation	35	The societies that have high long-term orientation want to create a future based on changes that are needed, while the ones with short-term orientation stick to the established norms in the society.
Indulgence vs restraint	70	Indulgent societies are generally more inclined to enjoy the natural human pleasures and wants.

The society in Denmark is low on power distance and generally more indulgent. This was in line with Samanta's experience when she was there. She also felt that in the work environment, they were more efficient and didn't waste time. The main takeaway she had from her time in Denmark was that it was important to observe and understand the values of whatever people group one was working with.

Expert View: Working in a 'Global Context', Egbert Schram

Egbert Schram is the global CEO of Hofstede Insights, a consulting firm that works on intercultural and organizational culture capabilities. The firm's insights are based on decades of research in the field by Greet Hofstede.

1. What are the cultural differences you see when working with clients across geographies?

Typically, a lack of ability/awareness/willingness to visualize culture and, in doing so, not understanding the impact of culture. Concrete examples are related to the six dimensions of national culture:

- Hierarchy in the wrong context.
- The inability to provide a sense of inclusion.
- Impatience in terms of time and communication, with too much focus on a decision as opposed to the decision-making process.
- Disagreement on the approach to building/leveraging structure.
- Disagreement on the concept of 'fluidity' and concepts such as pride vs development.
- Issues with regard to the level of formality and seriousness of business.

2. How can one build cultural competencies to work across boundaries?

First, by understanding that we, as groups of people, differ from one another. Secondly, by understanding that this difference is the concept for something beautiful, where we can learn from each other and use different approaches depending on the shifting contexts. Thirdly, by using a mental framework to encapsulate these differences in numbers, so discussions can become more objective (and less personal). And, finally, by objectifying differences, make better decisions while safeguarding inclusivity (people might still disagree with decisions you take, but at least now they will have a better understanding). For example, if an Indian is doing a negotiation with a Greek, looking at uncertainty avoidance, the average Greek scores 100 while an average Indian scores 40. It is possible that the Greek will like a high level of certainty in terms and be uncomfortable dealing with ambiguity. It is possible that trust will be low if there is no certainty; the way to build trust is to show certainty from the Indian's side.

3. How can one work more effectively in multinational/ cultural teams?

By creating a shared vision and agreement on explicit working practices within the team, taking into account that not everyone will always 'feel' happy with 'what' is being done and 'how' things are being done. Understanding the purpose and context builds more commitment. Ideally, you'd align the 'what' people do with 'how' they do it and 'how' it makes them feel. This would entail recruiting people who share certain value preferences (culture-fit), keeping in mind that too strong a culture (in a team) might lead to a lack of inclusivity of people who think and act differently.

'Consulting is all about solving client problems.' The partner speaking first in the induction programme spoke passionately about his topic as he shared some of his experiences of helping clients succeed. Samanta listened intently, thinking back on her internship and the excellent training she had received on how consulting projects worked. Now she was looking forward to taking a more hands-on approach as she moved into the next phase of learning the consulting trade. She would go from mostly observing and researching to practically using the knowledge she had received to that point. It was an exciting time for her.

After the induction ceremony, she received her first assignment. Hamid called to explain the new project she would be part of.

'There are only three of us working on this project. You, Tom, from the UK office, and me, as the engagement manager,' he said. 'The project is a small but interesting one. A UK cosmetics company wants an India strategy. It's a global brand and wants our advice on whether it should enter the Indian market, and, if they do, what its strategy should be.'

Samanta's heart jumped in her chest as she listened to Hamid. This project was going to test her skills, and mean a lot of valuable learning. It was also sobering to realize how important it was to select the correct course right away in helping the client. If they made a mistake at any phase of the project, there would be consequences. Hamid suggested that she follow the 'four-step method' in this project. The steps sounded simple as he explained them:

1. Understand: This step was to clearly understand the client requirements and set outcome expectations. While this might have already been articulated during the proposal and before winning the assignment, this

phase was an opportunity for the consultants to gain a better understanding of the needs and expectations of the client. This was also a time for the client to share more information about their expectations and priorities.

2. Research: In the research phase, the consultant was expected to gather relevant information through multiple sources that would help find a solution. The importance of research to consulting was that it made the solution data-driven. This phase also included discovering any similar problems that the firm had already solved in the past that could provide insight for the current problem. Finally, the research phase included the consultant engaging in discussions with the various stakeholders within the organization to understand their perspective.

3. Find solutions: The next step was to analyse the data and come up with potential solutions/recommendations for the client. This phase was where the consultant had the greatest opportunity to impact and serve the client.

4. Refine: The solution process was continuous, often requiring many revisions to finalize the solution. A consultant's success was in creating this buy-in with the client to sustain the relationship throughout the lengthy process.

Steps of Consulting

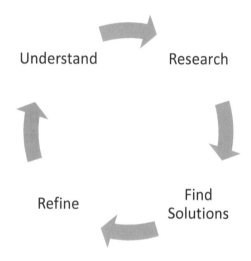

Samanta used this four-step method to evaluate the project, uncovering more information in the process. The UK company they were working with had entered Sri Lanka two years earlier and the project was being facilitated by a Pinnacle team from Singapore. The principal consultant working on the project had been Niramayan, a Sri Lankan consultant who worked out of the Singapore office. After working with the company for some time, the final strategy the consulting team had come up with was to franchise the brand to a local retail business leader, with guidance on brand and distribution. Though the roll-out was solid, with no major blunders, the company hadn't seen a big market for its product of premium natural cosmetics in its target marketplace.

Samanta and her team met Niramayan, who had a lot to share about how the senior leaders of the UK company thought. One major thing he mentioned, which, though not explicitly stated, was that the firm did not want to invest in a country if they didn't see the potential for an annual turnover of at least $25 million in three years. It was quite an ambitious growth target for any company in the industry.

After their meeting with Niramayan, Samanta, Tom and Hamid discussed how they should go about tackling the project. It was important to classify who the customers were and what the potential was in each of the segments. After selecting each of the segments, the next big question was whether the company should enter the Indian market. If they determined it was in the best interest of the company to enter the Indian market, the next step would be proposing the go-to market strategy. This included building the entire supply chain, brand positioning, marketing and people strategy. Quite a bit for a first project!

Samanta immersed herself in studying the industry and its dynamics. She carefully dissected each of the data points available for the industry and each of its various segments. In the meantime, Tom was in regular touch with the client team. They were excited about the potential they saw in the Indian market. Plus, they had seen some great successes from their competitors there.

The market data analysis showed that the industry was big enough to sustain many more companies. In fact, it appeared that even a niche player could easily see a potential of $25 million over three years. However, they knew that India was a complex country. There were many customer segments and the people most likely to spend on high-value cosmetics were largely limited to the upper middle and the upper classes.

After analysing the available industry data and market information, Samanta had a map of the solution diagrammed on a piece of paper so she could share it with the project team. She wanted everybody's buy-in before actually proposing a solution.

Target Segment	Middle Class and Upper Middle Class
Brand positioning	Natural, organic, safe, new and socially conscious.
Sourcing	Imported from the UK; source local ingredients from India wherever possible.
Pricing	Affordable premium.
Distribution	Independent outlets within premium mega retail stores and malls.
Target areas	Tier 1 cities, to start with.

After sharing her thoughts with the team, they discussed what she had presented. Hamid was happy with how Samanta was thinking. He bought into the framework Samanta was trying to create for the new brand. Tom, on the other hand, was sceptical.

'These guys want to create a unique space and pursue an ambitious plan,' he pointed out. 'Why can't they have solo outlets on streets in high-end neighbourhoods? That's how they operate in the UK.'

Samanta simply told him she didn't think that would work. Tom shrugged, still reluctant to accept her idea. Samanta shifted in her seat, uneasy about how things were going. The client had given them a good brief and they were in line with their ambitions. If Tom didn't agree with or believe in the plan, he wasn't going to be able to present it with conviction to the client.

After the meeting, she had a talk with Hamid. 'What should we do now?' she said.

Hamid shrugged. 'Think first principles here, Sammy. Show Tom the data and evidence that back up the plan. He's not going to present a solution to the client built solely on the hunch of a new consultant.'

Samanta knew he was right. She sat down to compile the data. She found information on the spending propensity of customers that might go to premium malls. At a few of the malls, footfall data was also available. She identified comparable competition and how they were faring in the market. Many of them had their stores in malls and a few had them in high-end neighbourhoods as well.

After she was finished, she sat back and smiled. Now Tom could study the data and experience the market for himself. It was something she realized was critical when trying to influence others and sell your ideas. She nodded to herself. It was an important lesson to learn so early in her career. The success principle that Hamid had mentioned to her months ago came to mind: 'Build the coalition that will make you successful!'

* * *

It wasn't easy to build a plan for the client. There were a lot of variables involved in making a brand successful in India. The product, price, location and positioning were all critical elements that had to be considered. Samanta wondered how they were going to launch.

When they met next, Samanta explained her approach to Tom clearly. In just under two minutes, she summed up her solution. The power of an 'elevator speech' was something she had started believing in after her coaching from Jacob.

Tom was open to her ideas, but wanted to make sure they had a data-based approach and a few options to present to the client before choosing the final solution. Hamid had a different point of view. He wasn't so sure about providing the client with multiple options. He wanted the team to discuss the various options internally and provide the best solution to the client based on the data they had collected.

'We have a good idea of the market. Let's have a better idea of the client,' he said.

The next step was to interview the client's key stakeholders. They could have taken this step earlier, since all the effort they had put in this far could have been futile if the client had had a different point of view. But they had decided to wait until after their exhaustive secondary round of research and formation of their initial solution to talk to the stakeholders and hope for the best.

While Samanta was part of client interactions during the internship, it was critical that she play a more independent role here. It was also important to do it right. During the induction, one of the principal consultants had given them an exhaustive training on how to conduct client meetings and interviews. She had provided a list of five considerations to help ensure a great interview. They were:

1. *Understand the context:* Have a good idea of the company, the latest happenings and a good understanding of the interviewee.
   - Tips: Go through its website, newspaper articles and reports available. Check out any public profiles that are available as well, such as on LinkedIn or other publicly shared networking sites.
2. *Confident introduction:* Introduce yourself, your team and tell them why you are there and what is expected during the meeting. Try to build rapport right at the beginning.
   - Tips: Discuss common connections and maybe discuss some non-business aspects.
3. *Listen intently:* Don't make the client uncomfortable by being distracted or by not acknowledging their points. Your body language should be open and your interest and intent to listen evident.

- Tips: Take notes, acknowledge the points, make eye contact and maybe even lean forward to show your full engagement.
4. *Handle interviewees right:* Not all interviewees will show as much interest as you do. This could be due to something going on in their own life, or their like or dislike of you, the consultant. They may also genuinely be upset by the consulting firm itself. It is important that the interviewer understand these dynamics but not lose focus on the objective.
   - Tips: Acknowledge the issues but do not make comments that may have a negative impact on the client or the consulting firm.
5. *Manage the flow:* Every meeting has time constraints. Therefore, it is important to stay focused and keep the interview moving, making sure to ask the most relevant questions, and for necessary clarification from the interviewee.
   - Tips: Plan your questions before the interview. Make note of all the key aspects to be covered/not covered at different points of the interview, so nothing is missed.

The consultant had also shared a model used by interrogators but said that was effective in other contexts as well. It was called the PEACE model (see next page).

P: Plan and prepare	Gather the important facts and plan the approach.
E: Engage and explain	Introduce, set expectations and outline objectives.
A: Account, Clarify and Challenge	Probe the topic more deeply and ask clarifying questions to gain a fuller understanding.
C: Close	Close the meeting and share next steps, if necessary.
E: Evaluate	Evaluate the major themes after the interview and document the important information.

Tom and Samanta took some time to interview the CEO for the South Asian region, the CMO of the client, the CFO and the business leader who was proposed to be the CEO of the India region. Samanta found what the client had in mind interesting. But what surprised her was her ability to ask each person meaningful questions, keep them interested during the interview and gain insight into what the team was thinking about its India strategy. It was clear that her training was paying off.

There were a lot of remote discussions with internal consultants and client representatives across various geographies. Hamid had given a few tips to Samanta to help her be effective in remote meetings.

1. Be confident, have the right tone and a positive body language. Have a short introduction and get to know each other.
2. Lead the meeting (since she was facilitating the interviews/ discussions). Set a clear agenda and points of discussion.

3. Ensure the basics are clear (sound is clear and audible, the video is kept on, and remember to take notes).
4. Send questions in advance if required and send minutes of the discussion for any clarifications/changes.
5. Make it engaging—by probing, clarifying, appreciating and reiterating what was shared. An important tip here is to have the video properly aligned and not being distracted during the discussions. It is important to let the other person know that you are listening intently.

The client was eager to establish its presence within the customer segments that ranked highest in affluence and discretionary spending on cosmetics. Samanta designated these segments as the 'urban emerging affluent' and the 'classic affluent'. The client also wanted to target the traditional urban upper middle class in the country. They were the group the client thought would be willing to try natural cosmetic products that had a Western brand associated with them.

The next month was spent data-crunching, conducting primary research with potential customers, market testing and formulating the solution. Samanta also took the liberty to contact consultants who had experience in the industry to see what advice they could offer. One of them made an interesting observation—the Indian market wanted variety. It didn't want another same old product. He suggested creating different product varieties that were centred on the main products. He said this would make customers come to the stores more often to purchase these varieties. While she was listening, Samanta remembered something the client had mentioned. They wanted to introduce a limited set of products in the country first to test the market before looking at the results and adjusting from there. But in light of what the consultant was suggesting, she wondered if that approach would kill the market entry.

After many deliberations, a plan for entering the market was completed. The client would position their brand of cosmetics as natural but modern, and moderately premium, so that customers from several segments could have access to them. Distribution would take place through company outlets in upper-class malls in metros and select cities in the country. Samanta insisted that a plan be included to keep innovating and introducing a new product every six months, at least, to keep the customers interested. Personalized selling and product trials were how marketing worked. And the risk was significantly diminished, since the recommendations were substantiated by considerable amounts of research and data.

After considering every angle with the help of the consulting team, the client made the final decision to open twenty outlets in the country. Over the next four years, Samanta kept tabs on how the company was doing, and watched as they became a well-established player in the market with a unique position in the industry.

Samanta found that this first project taught her many things about the different aspects of consulting. Things such as how to engage with clients, interviewing skills, working with a team and other stakeholders, creating a hypothesis, data analysis and crafting a solution, to name a few. The most important lesson she learnt was that a solution was always dependent on the client. The solution that had worked for one client might not work for another with similar needs. Something that helped her understand this was thinking of a great consultant as a great actor. An actor could play different characters in various movies, but there was an underlying distinctiveness that was unique only to him/her.

One of the fundamental aspects of consulting that she got exposed to at Pinnacle was project-management skills. The project effectiveness and profitability depends on how this estimation is done. For example, each element of the project may require effort from various levels of consultants. The table below illustrates how the efforts get distributed. For example, if it is diagnosis discussions with key stakeholders, the interviews might be distributed with the various project team members.

Project Stage	Details	Partner (Hours @$200)	Director (Hours @$150)	Manager (Hours @$100)	Consultant (Hours @$50)
Diagnosis	Discussions with key stakeholders	5	8	10	
	Secondary research of available data			8	40

Pinnacle had elaborate mechanisms to look at effort estimation—the man-hours of various levels of consultants involved in the project and the time required completing various phases. This was well encoded and the seniors in the team helped her put the project plan together. However, she learnt quite a bit more than what was written in the plan while executing the project. Some of the interesting ones were:

1. Clients do not work at your pace. Some stakeholders are faster than you and some are slower. You need to adjust your style to ensure timely information and outputs from them.

2. Some of the team members are prompt and follow timelines. Others you have to nudge to ensure that the project outputs are a priority for them. The use of various project management/tracking tools such as GANTT charts helps to bring a structured approach to the same.

3. Follow a no-surprise policy—ensure communication flows to all stakeholders involved. Reviews with the client and communication with the team members on what is going on is critical for a concerted effort.

4. Scope management. If you are handling a project, ensure that the scope is adhered to. While the client would like you to do far more than what is there in the scope, it is important to realize that effort and time management are important aspects of a project's success.

5. Perfection dilemma. Often, the perfect solution might not be the most pragmatic. It is important to realize that time is an important factor for a project's success. A delayed project may often lose its strategic value.

The whole experience was definitely a huge success for Samanta and she felt good about what she had accomplished. Hamid took every opportunity to announce to others the great work she had done. Tom's praise was also very high. Samanta was a sought-after consultant for many similar projects from then on. Pinnacle wasn't a place that tolerated mediocrity. If a project went poorly, often, the consultants who had worked on it had a tough time getting other projects after that. Samanta figured that was the culture at Pinnacle, and the price to be paid for working at a firm that valued success so highly. It was something that Samanta got used to very fast.

5

Growing Up

Going from a consultant to a director was not easy. Samanta had worked with more than seventy clients across the globe during the time. She built strong teams and was seen as a person who could be trusted with the key assignments of the firm. Over the past eight years, growing from a consultant to a director, she went through some of the key choices and experiences that characterized her growth:

1. To execute or to build.
2. The golden rules to lead.
3. A man's world.
4. The change agent.

To Execute or to Build

In the next three years after joining Pinnacle, Samanta continued to learn and eventually became a senior consultant. She gained considerable experience in market-entry strategies and sales-force effectiveness. She started working closely with Aekta around this time as well. A graduate of the Wharton School of Business, Aekta was a partner at Pinnacle and a force to be reckoned with in the firm. After becoming a partner within seven years of signing on with the company, she commanded the attention of CEOs of clients for her expertise and ambition.

After a meeting, Samanta and Aekta started chatting.

'Why don't you focus on market-entry strategies?' Aekta said. 'Build your identity as a thought leader and an expert in the field, and become a global resource.'

Samanta liked the idea. It was definitely a way to grow in the firm.

'You would be interacting with teams from Europe and North America who are working with clients interested in Asian market-entry strategies,' she continued. 'You could even work with clients from India itself who want to enter developed markets.'

The scope was huge. If she wanted to do this, she would have to focus on three or four industry sectors. She would also have to build the capabilities and a lot of effort would go into it. There would be countless hours of research, and concentrated time working with industry leaders for at least six months. It would mean taking a break from active consulting for a while.

She thought it over more and talked it over with Hamid.

'These are detours on your journey to becoming a partner,' he said. 'Why would you waste time doing some research and talking to random people when there are prestigious client assignments waiting for you?'

As she walked away from the meeting, she couldn't help but be discouraged. Two people she highly respected were giving her contradicting advice regarding a career-changing decision. Hamid had a point about slamming the brakes on her career as a thought leader if she chose to take this new route. But Aekta made some good points too.

'These assignments will keep coming,' she had pointed out. 'Nobody's going to forget you in six months. If you work on a special assignment such as this and build your identity as a thought leader, you'll be an even greater asset to the firm. Think of it as going into hibernation to survive the future.'

Samanta genuinely liked working with teams. She found that her team members challenged her, and working with them gave her energy. She would miss it if she decided to pursue this new path. It would also be hard saying no to most of new projects popping up, so she could focus on her training.

It was around this time that she had met Ivan at a board meeting. A senior managing partner for the European region, he was considered a god in the consulting realm at Pinnacle. And he had the reputation of spending 50 per cent of his time mentoring young consultants—a choice he made before retiring from active consulting. He now serves as adviser to CEOs and boards of various companies in an independent capacity.

Samanta decided to meet Ivan. As they talked, she was pleased to find he was a genuinely warm person without any air of superiority from what he had achieved over the years. And he had achieved a lot. He had climbed from his humble beginnings as an associate to a managing partner in one of the most profitable regions in all of Pinnacle. He had gleaned vast stores of experience along the way as well.

Samanta shared her background and experience with Ivan. She also told him her dilemma, hoping he could give her some insight into what she should do next. He looked thoughtful for a moment and then responded. 'As far as I know you, you've gained considerable skills in project and client management,' he said. 'Even though there's no way to excel in it, building your expertise in an area you're passionate about is a gift in itself. Since we're in the knowledge business, if you have more knowledge than those around you, they'll respect you and you'll always be seen as an asset.' He stroked his chin. 'I wouldn't say taking this new path is a detour— I'd say it's like stopping at a gas station to fill up before a long trip. I'd have to go with Aekta on this.'

Becoming a thought leader in market-entry strategies wasn't easy. First, she had to fully understand how the firm helped the client through the services it provided. Then, she would have to determine what unique value Pinnacle offered beyond what the competition did, and figure out how to express that to the client.

Aekta mentored Samanta during this process, providing insight when needed, but never taking away her sense of responsibility.

'Look, Sammy, you have to do the work yourself. Talk to the partners and principal consultants involved in market-entry strategies. Talk to our clients who have successfully entered different markets, and ask what to watch out for. They'll give you valuable insight.'

Aekta was right. The market-entry-strategy projects she had done as part of her training had hardly taught her anything compared to the wealth of knowledge she gleaned from the partners and clients. The only issue she faced was deciding how to divide her time between creating white papers and compiling the knowledge she had gained for the firm to refer to.

Samanta spoke to more than fifteen partners and principal consultants who had done similar projects, combing through their documentation for deeper insight. She also talked to more than a dozen client partners. They had a wealth of information on how Pinnacle's recommendations had affected them, both positively and negatively. Based on the information she gathered, she co-authored an article with Aekta on what the potential reasons for failure could be when expanding to an Asian economy from North America.

They wrote a second article a short time later on why organizations shouldn't try to force-fit their home market strategies to Asian markets. Both articles were published in a famous management magazine. It was also published internally in Pinnacle's magazine, which was circulated to their clients around the globe.

The articles received immediate response. Two clients they had worked with earlier reached out to them for engagements regarding market-entry strategies. Three enquiries came in from Fortune 500 companies seeking Pinnacle's help in crafting their strategies.

Samanta and Aekta found that they had become sought-after consultants in the field. Samanta realized that the time she had taken to research and write the articles had been well worth it and had helped her expand her borders. She felt refreshed and more confident in her ability to add value to the firm.

'Every now and then, we have to do something in our career beyond the day-to-day,' Aekta said. 'It helps us reinvent ourselves. Otherwise, the routine takes over and we stagnate.'

Samanta couldn't have agreed more.

The Golden Rules to Lead

Samanta was in her third year at Pinnacle when she started taking the lead on projects. She had a project manager under her, but as a senior consultant, she was in charge of the major project components, including bringing the new consultants who joined the team up to speed.

Overseeing projects brought a whole new list of challenges. She had to learn how to manage the team under her. This included highlighting the three major aspects of consulting: meeting tight deadlines on client projects, continuously striving for improvement and being willing to make personal sacrifices.

She also had to deal with another factor in her new role. The bright sparks who joined the company every year were often conditioned to work hard by the B-schools they attended, but sometimes acted as lone wolves. Samanta's role was to help them channel their individual brilliance into a team effort that produced the kind of outstanding results Pinnacle required.

Samanta was a no-nonsense leader. When she was responsible for getting something done, she made sure it was done with excellence. This meant that she required her team to work at their most proficient level. Hard deadlines abounded, and flawless execution was her daily requirement. Mistakes were not tolerated and she ensured that everything leaving her desk was the best it could be. She had no patience for those less talented or hard-working than herself.

After becoming the project manager, she asked three of the team members to leave the firm due to poor performance. This led to the partners assigning only the best team members to her, assuming that anyone less capable wouldn't be able to meet her expectations.

In a team engagement survey, the comments stated things such as 'Sammy is a great consultant. I wonder if she could also become a great manager. I love working under her for the training I'm receiving, but it's like trying to live near the Sun'; 'I wish she was a bit more considerate. We all have our low points and challenges'; and 'Sammy is the best consultant out there. She has amazing knowledge and intellect. I look forward to learning from her.'

The comments from the reports came as a surprise to Samanta. She had always thought of herself as a great manager. She decided to talk to Ivan about it.

Ivan started by drawing circles pertaining to roles on a piece of paper.

'You are transitioning from the role of managing yourself to managing those around you,' he said. 'You are also gaining insight into managing business.' He pointed out each circle as he drew them. 'While you're good at managing yourself and getting things done, you'll need to grow in your ability to manage others, especially those in your team.'

Managing
Self

Managing
Others

Managing
Business

'You know,' he said, looking at the ceiling. 'You remind me of myself back in the day.' He glanced at her and smiled. 'I was driven, passionate and always demanded the highest performance from my team. Mediocrity wasn't tolerated.' He looked at her squarely. 'There's nothing wrong with that, Sammy. But when it comes to talent, not everyone is cast from the same stone. A good leader needs to shape his or her team based on the strengths available to them.'

She nodded. What he said made sense.

Ivan continued. 'There are two other critical aspects to this that helped me become the sought-after leader I am today. The first is the Pygmalion effect.'

Samanta was familiar with the character from Greek mythology and had even heard the term bounced around in the business world, but she was unsure of what the concept stood for.

'The Pygmalion effect has to do with a highly impactful social phenomenon that extensive research has uncovered,' Ivan explained. 'The primary researchers were Rosenthal and Jacobsen, who discovered that in an educational setting, teachers' expectations of their students tended to become a self-fulfilling prophecy. That is, if the teachers had high expectations and believed their students could achieve something, more often than not, they could. On the other hand, if they had low expectations, the results would reflect that. Essentially, positive expectations influence positive performance, and negative expectations influence negative performance.'

He glanced at her to see if she was following what he was saying. She nodded.

'I've experienced that myself,' she said. 'I usually form my impression of a team member within the first day or two, and then whatever happens after that validates my initial impression and expectations. I think I understand what you're saying I need to be cautious about my impressions and then setting expectations accordingly. This is great advice. I can help individuals perform better by tuning my expectations.'

'Good,' said Ivan. 'The second aspect involves the power of inquiry. Now, from what I know of you so far Sammy, you're a live wire, full of energy and zest. But,' he said, holding up a finger, 'that can also mean a judgmental attitude and impatience with those less dynamic than you. That's where you need to employ the power of inquiry. You use it all the time with your clients, but consultants often forget this important tool when dealing with their own teams.'

Samanta nodded. She had to admit she was much more prone to be patient with her clients than her teammates.

'You're right,' she said. 'Though I feel it's because I don't have time to ask questions, understand and then explain. I just tell them what to do, so we can get the project done.'

'I understand that,' said Ivan. 'But the only thing that will help you become a better leader is your ability to ask the right questions, and the patience to truly listen to the answers. This will generate ownership and help you connect with your team.' He looked her right in the eye. 'The only thing holding you back from being a great manager is your listening skills.'

Samanta had to chuckle at his bluntness. But he was right, and she was happy to receive such honest feedback. She certainly didn't want to work with a team that didn't believe in her as a leader.

'I can see the value of what you're saying,' she said. 'And these are the golden rules to live by in this industry. I promise I'll follow them to the best of my abilities.'

As she transitioned to an even more intense leadership role, she faced many new challenges. She had to start managing multiple teams as she led various projects. Within these teams, there were some team members that stayed for several years but most were transitional. They would work under her for three or four months before joining other projects. The one thing that they all had in common were their skills and their knowledge of the industry.

Apart from the golden rules Ivan had taught her, Samanta formed her own model for being a great leader that she called the 'Golden Circle'.

While the Pygmalion effect and the power of inquiry helped Samanta adjust her attitude and hone her skills, the Golden Circle gave her the principles she needed to grow as a great manager in the years to come. It would help her make the leap from a fantastic individual contributor to a people's leader.

Building Trust

'Sammy, we're all pretty upset about what happened yesterday,' said Dhan, an associate working on Samanta's team. 'You didn't speak up for us in front of the partner.'

Samanta scanned the group of team members gathered around her. They were all watching this exchange between her and Dhan. She glanced at him. He looked a little embarrassed now, but his jaw was set and he looked her straight in the eye. She definitely hadn't expected this when she came into work this morning.

The day before had been brutal. After weeks of working their tails off on a project for an impatient client, they had given a prep presentation to one of the partners of the firm. He wasn't happy with their progress and had complained to Samanta that the team wasn't putting in the effort to meet the client's expectations, no matter how unrealistic. Samanta had held her tongue, not wanting to get in an argument with an irate partner. She had another meeting directly after the presentation, so, after a curt nod of acknowledgement to the partner, she had left.

Now, Dhan stood staring at her with that disapproving look as the rest of the team watched. Samanta knew now that she hadn't been fair to the team. After all their hard work, she hadn't defended them against the partner's accusations. Maybe once she would have told them to just live with it and stop acting like children, but she now understood the importance of hearing them out.

'You're right, Dhan,' she said, knowing she was really addressing the entire room of teammates. 'I didn't want to confront the partner when he was in that mood, since it wouldn't have proved anything. However, it wasn't fair to you, and I will definitely stand up for you in future, if that's what you want. You worked incredibly hard, and there's no doubt about that. But keep in mind that our effectiveness isn't measured in hours but in the relevance of our outcomes. You would have received a similar response from any partner. But I know it was important to show that I supported you, and that's something I'll work on in future.'

One of the biggest things Samanta had learnt was the importance of being transparent. She realized that admitting her shortcomings didn't erode the team's trust. In fact, it was often just the opposite. It helped them see her as part of the team—the first among equals. And in that role, she saw the importance of being an advocate for them as well.

There were four principles Samanta followed that helped her build trust with her team:

1. A team leader should always work on one's competence. Competence has a direct impact on credibility, especially with regard to knowledge work. A high-calibre team will never trust or want to work with a manager who is incompetent.
2. One should always be open about one's shortcomings. If one didn't know something, it was best to try learning it from wherever one can. Teams love to see a growth mindset in their leaders, as opposed to a fixed one.
3. One should always be genuine and say only what one really meant. It was important to avoid breaking promises as much as possible, as this eroded trust faster than anything else.
4. It was crucial to show respect. Even when things were going wrong, being in control of one's emotions was paramount. Emotions should not control a team leader, but the other way around.

While there were moments Samanta strayed from these principles, she strove to make them defining characteristics of her identity as an authentic leader.

Making Oneself and Others Better Every Day

'True nobility is being superior to your former self'

—Ernest Hemingway

Samanta sat across from the vice president of a large pharmaceutical firm. KK, a highly respected senior partner at Pinnacle, sat next to her. This was an important meeting, and this a high-value client. Hence KK's presence. Samanta was on the verge of becoming an engagement manager and was confident with clients at this stage in her career, but it was nice to have KK there regardless. He was well known in consulting circles and knew who was who in the industry.

KK asked Samanta to start the meeting by giving some background to the client. She did so, sharing point by point the objectives of the assignment and what the purpose of the meeting was. As she explained, the vice president nodded his understanding.

KK took over after she was finished. He chatted about different events that had occurred in the industry and asked questions to glean the vice president's view on the problems his company was facing. Samanta marvelled at how natural he came across as—a perfect mix of professional and informal. He and the vice president even shared a few laughs.

After the meeting, Samanta pulled KK aside to ask about his conversation style.

'How did you establish such a good relationship in such a short time?' she said.

'The main thing is, I always position the other person as an equal in my mind. I seek partnership, and for that reason, I get it.' He shrugged. 'It's always "we" in the conversation, and never "you" and "us". And even if I'm talking to a CEO or a managing director, I do my best to relax with them, enjoying the conversation from my heart. I try to avoid just focusing on the "mind"—the stats and strategies—and try to understand the people themselves.'

Throughout the next few months, Samanta realized that every day of work was an opportunity to learn from and understand others. Mostly they were informal conversations but they gave her a whole new breadth of experience. She found that, in the past, it was easy to fall into the mindset of 'I know it all'. With her impressive educational background, prestigious job with one of the best consulting firms in the world and reputation as a sought-after consultant for multimillion-dollar assignments, it was easy to fall on the side of arrogance instead of humility.

A book that made a significant impact on her outlook was *Mindset: The New Psychology of Success* by Carol S. Dweck.[1] Throughout the book, Dweck unpacked the concept of a growth mindset versus a fixed mindset. With a fixed mindset, people believed that their potential, such as intelligence or talent, were fixed traits. They also tended to view themselves in absolute terms. Either they were good at something or not. With a growth mindset, however, people believed their potential could be developed. There was always something to learn and always ways to improve.

Since reading the book, Samanta's focus became helping herself and others develop a growth mindset. She had an analogy she enjoyed sharing with her team to drive the point home.

'Imagine you're sick, so you go to see a doctor. However, it comes to your attention that this doctor isn't aware of modern developments in his or her field. Would you still go to

---

[1]   C.S. Dweck, *Mindset: The New Psychology of Success*, Random House Digital, Inc., 2008.

him or her for healthcare advice? While confidence and belief
in our own capabilities are important, a growth mindset helps
us continue to improve in every area. Pretend we're those
doctors. Would others want to consult with us if they knew
how uninformed we were?'

An instance when Samanta had to face this issue in
someone else occurred when a young consultant started
sharing her biased views of clients with the rest of the team.
During the initial phase of interacting with a client, it was
important that the consultant keep an open mind and not
form opinions. This young consultant was undermining that
by spreading her opinions. Samanta tried addressing the issue
by giving indirect feedback but the consultant only tried to
justify her conclusions. It was clear that the consultant needed
to change her attitude if she wanted to continue growing
in the industry. However, Samanta had learnt the value of
keeping the responsibility on the team member instead of
simply demanding change.

Earlier in her career, Samanta's practice had been to give
feedback in public. She had learnt since that it made people
defensive. She decided to take the consultant out to coffee
to spend time with her and understand her better. She was
curious to find out why the consultant felt the need to make
judgemental statements. What she discovered surprised her.

'Sammy, we all look up to you,' the consultant said.
'You've set the bar so high, and I'm just trying to look like I
know what I'm talking about in front of you to impress you.
And others too, I guess.'

'And what impression does making those comments give
others?' Samanta said.

The girl stared at the ceiling for a moment. 'Maybe they
think I'm ahead of the curve? That I'm reading the clients
accurately after only a brief interaction?'

Samanta shrugged. 'Could be. Is that what you would think if a teammate made similar comments to you?'

The consultant looked down at her coffee. 'Probably not. I would think they were being a know-it-alls and overly critical.'

'Okay,' said Samanta. She knew she had to be careful here. The consultant was getting the idea that maybe she wasn't as good a consultant as she thought she was. However, Samanta wanted her to change without becoming demotivated. She wanted to tap into the consultant's need to feel respected. She pulled out a piece of paper and started drawing up a plan:

Need	To be a great consultant who is respected by peers and seniors.
Derailing behaviour	Lack of quality analysis and quick to draw conclusions.
Change plan	Have all data in place, analyse data and base decisions on data. Have a critical-thinking mindset.
Support	Be mentored by Samanta and learn from other successful consultants.

Samanta concluded the discussion with these nuggets of wisdom, 'A critical thinker is able to deduce consequences from what she knows, and she knows how to make use of information to solve problems and seek relevant sources of information to inform herself. Critical thinking should not be confused with being argumentative or critical of other people. Although critical-thinking skills can be used in exposing fallacies and bad reasoning, critical thinking can also play an important role in cooperative reasoning and constructive tasks. Critical thinking can help us acquire knowledge, improve our theories and strengthen arguments. We can use critical thinking to enhance work processes and improve social institutions.'

Once the consultant recognized her derailing behaviours, Samanta asked her to think about what she needed to do to change. The consultant came up with the better part of the plan herself and mentioned her need for support from Samanta. Samanta nodded in satisfaction. The consultant had taken responsibility for her own change. Samanta had simply acted as a mirror.

Samanta told her to read about the aspects of critical thinking and apply it to a real case they were working on. Within a couple of days, the consultant was able to bring a gist of what it was and where she was lacking. 'I know I always need to gather more information, improve my understanding of the problem and strengthen my arguments with relevant logic and concepts,' she said. 'I read an interesting article by Richard Paul and Linda Elder,[2] and found that some of the mistakes that I am making are exactly what they have pointed out. I have been jumping to conclusions and may also be arriving at unreasonable conclusions. This really needs to change if I have to become a better professional. I found all the four recommendations from them to improve critical thinking relevant: "Clarify your thinking", "Stick to the point", "Question the questions" and "Be reasonable". I think, for me, the most important is "Be reasonable". I should build my own logic reasoning and listen to others' logic as well. I need to be more reasonable—going by logical arguments rather than my own judgements. I will try to make this change, and it would be helpful if you could guide me in case I deviate.'

It was a relief for Samanta to hear this from the consultant.

---

[2] R. Paul and L. Elder, 'Learning the Art of Critical Thinking', *Rotman Management Magazine*, January 2014, pp. 40–45.

Improving One's Critical Thinking: Recommendations by Richard Paul and Linda Elder

1. *Clarify your thinking:* The process of making your thoughts clear, noting it down and expressing it to others in a way it is mutually understood.
2. *Stick to the point:* The ability to stay focused on the problem rather than wandering with fragmented thoughts that may not have logical connections.
3. *Question the questions:* The ability to ask powerful questions. A good critical thinker is able to ask the right questions to have a holistic understanding of the situation. Often out of habit, the questions become limited or, often, certain types of questions are not asked. It is important to introspect on this aspect.
4. *Be reasonable:* The ability to question one's own logic, change one's stance if required and be open to others' points of view.

As Samanta continued to learn about the growth mindset, she discovered that improvement was simply a blend of keeping a learner's attitude forefront and creating opportunities to encourage learning. She realized that her job as a leader was to help others understand their blind spots and provide them with learning opportunities. The opportunities could take many forms. It could be as simple as sharing knowledge, assigning a new task, a project or a client presentation, or even encouraging research in a specific area. However, behavioural change required much more coaching, as well as a willingness to change on the part of the offending party. Many times, Samanta shared her own stories of change to help break down the walls young consultants had built to look more competent in front of their peers and seniors.

Helping Others Thrive

John started working with Samanta for the first time when she started leading projects independently, as a manager of projects. He was a senior consultant and had been in the firm fewer years than her. Samanta admired his extraordinary mind and the speed at which he completed his work. He was always at the top of his class when it came to delivering on projects.

However, what he lacked was the ability to engage in informal conversations with the clients, or even his fellow team members.

Samanta knew she had the right blend of impressive delivery capabilities and engagement skills. She observed that John, however, was generally silent around her unless they were having a discussion on deliverables. Samanta wondered whether or not he would ever reach his full potential at Pinnacle. She even began wondering why he had been hired in the first place. Pinnacle generally hired consultants with exceptional confidence and communication skills.

One day, Samanta noticed Aekta having a one-on-one discussion with John. The surprising part was it went on for nearly half the day. It was rare for a senior partner such as Aekta to be spending that kind of time with a senior consultant.

Samanta approached Aekta after she had finished her conversation and asked what she thought of John.

'He's one of the best minds here, Sammy,' she said. 'He's the future of the firm. Organizations are looking at digital transformation and trying to find ways to manage that transition. If there is one person I rely on for advice in that area, it's John.'

Samanta decided she needed to get to know John better. It was clear to her now that behind the veil of a dull, introverted personality was the highly intelligent mind of an expert.

After talking to him, it was obvious that he understood the challenges many companies faced and how digital transformation could help address them. She felt that CEOs or top management teams would be excited to hear what he had to say if they understood how much it would help them.

His interesting take brought to mind a session she had attended on personality differences at work. The facilitator had used an instrument called Myers-Briggs Type Indicator, or MBTI. Samanta's type had been ESTJ, or Extroversion, Sensing, Thinking and Judging. It indicated that Samanta gained energy by interacting with others and was generally extroverted in these interactions, that she took in information based on her five senses, processed information based on logic and data, and liked order and predictability. However, based on her understanding of this tool, she wondered if John could be more of an INTJ—Introverted, Intuitive, Thinking and Judging.

Samanta realized she needed to appreciate the different personalities of her teammates and the strengths they brought to the group. Although the company itself might lean towards certain type of personalities, the skills and talents of each team member were what mattered. It was important for her to leverage each of their strengths for the benefit of the team as a whole.

In her efforts to help others thrive, she learnt it was important to recognize that each person had a unique personality and set of strengths and weaknesses, and that a good leader leverages this for the benefit of all.

Building Ownership

Samanta found that, as a rule, most consultants struggled with being stretched by timelines and deliverables. This resulted in the constant juggling of multiple tasks and assignments. Often, the project manager was the one to set the timeline and deliverables as per the project plan. This also meant that the project manager was the one pushing the team to meet deadlines.

A manager Samanta looked up to was Aekta. Many other consultants felt the same way. She was enjoyable to work with and was known as an exceptional leader, with words such as 'inspiring', 'motivating', 'engaging' and 'coach' popping up to describe her. Samanta was able to talk to her whenever she had difficult problems regarding a project, which was something that made her appreciate Aekta even more.

Aekta always listened patiently and asked questions to help Samanta determine the best solution. She would often push Samanta to think about possibilities as well. If she couldn't come up with anything, Aekta would invite other team members into the conversation to get their input. If that didn't work, she would provide a few suggestions but always leave it to the team to decide what it wanted to ultimately do.

After a few of these meetings, Samanta realized that Aekta could have given her genius solutions right off the bat. But she never did.

'Why don't you just give me the solution up front?' Samanta asked her during one of their meetings. 'I know you have ideas of what we could do to address the problems we're facing.'

Aekta smiled. 'Why hire smart people and then tell them what to do? Let them figure it out.'

Samanta couldn't argue with that logic. It created a strong sense of ownership among the team members, since they were the ones coming up with the solutions. Samanta shared with

Aekta some of the principles that she used with her team to build ownership:

1. Work on the Pygmalion effect: Trust the team to deliver its best.
2. Explain the why: Why they were given the job, why it mattered to the team, client and organization, and why it was given to this team in particular.
3. Build the 'peaking zone' *(see below)*.
4. Do not micromanage: Let the team figure out how to get things done.
5. Provide appreciation and constructive feedback as needed.

Building the 'peaking zone' was an interesting aspect that Samanta refined over time. The 'peaking zone' was an area of maximized work output, learning and energy of the team members. Performance and motivation went up tenfold in the period! Samanta observed that the ability to keep herself and others in the zone was the biggest enabler to peak performance.

Different zones of individual performance:

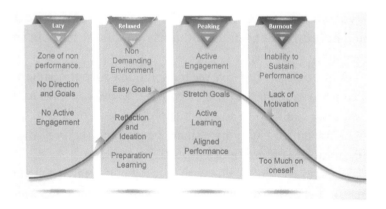

The consultants who delivered their best often operated in the peaking zone. It is the state of being in active engagement. Samanta learnt about this concept when she was doing an assignment with a large FMCG organization. Her assignment involved building a high-performance organization, and it meant quite a bit of culture change. The new CEO, who was focusing on this change, was a well-known figure in the industry and was respected for what he had achieved in his career. Samanta remembered what he had told her: 'I want my key team members to be in their peak performance at least 50 per cent of their work hours. I believe this can be done only through inspiring and stretch goals, and everybody working together to achieve it.'

It led to a set of insightful discussions with the client leadership team and evolving a change plan that involved desired leadership mindsets, performance management practices and skill-building for leaders on how they could activate their peak performance.

At Pinnacle, Samanta had seen teams that worked really hard, so much so that many of them burnt out. She wanted to avoid this for sustained performance. The trick was to allow the team to be in the relaxed performance zone once in a while. This also involved active timeouts, ensuring that somebody who was showing behaviours of a burnout was allowed to relax or promised timeout soon. The team members were in a state of energized performance attained through learning, challenging tasks, collaboration and personalized guidance, keeping them in the zone of peak performance. In the zone of peak performance, the team members are at their best, and this is the secret sauce of teams that bring the best outcomes.

Samanta had a secret formula based on three questions to help identify the zone of peak performance for herself and her team members:

1. Do I really enjoy what I am doing, or do I just think 'it's part of the job'?
2. Am I bringing in new ways of doing things and in a process of continuous improvement, or doing what is 'required'?
3. Is there a feeling of 'stretch' and 'active learning', or is it business as usual?

The ultimate experience of being in the zone that Samanta could relate to was while being in the fencing tournaments. Agility, focus and the desire to perform the best were unbeaten while in the game. She had seen that in some of the projects where the team members were so involved in their work that time and effort never mattered.

Building Influence

Something Samanta learnt quickly was that influence was a key trait of leadership. Without influence, the chances of a leader or a manager turning their plans into reality were low. It was a turnaround CEO that taught her some of the key components to building influence. He had gained his insight through his experience turning around three companies.

The CEO had hired Pinnacle to help him make his company's sales organization more efficient and market-oriented. It was a tough decision for the company to make, as they were already operating at a loss, and hiring Pinnacle was expensive. But the CEO had convinced the board to hire Pinnacle and had set high standards for the outcome of the project.

Samanta had witnessed him speaking to key stakeholders, the board, employee groups and customers. What stood out for her was his deep conviction. In a conversation they had later, she asked him about it.

'If I don't believe in the decision, how will the employees and other stakeholders believe? Creating belief is the act of influence. For belief to happen, you need to have deep conviction about the idea yourself. Then everything works out.'

The second component of influence she learnt from the CEO revolved around doing by oneself what one was asking others to do.

'The moment the team feels you are out of touch, they will take you for granted,' he said. 'For example, unless you have made a tough sale yourself or been part of a difficult customer discussion, you're never going to earn the respect of your sales team. Your influence is always enhanced by the critical experiences you've had. The conviction to propose an idea, influence key stakeholders and see the idea come to fruition will only happen if you are building it up with your experiences and are willing to get your hands dirty.'

The third element he touched upon was credibility.

'A leader without credibility can't make things happen. Credibility comprises the three Cs—competence, consistency and care. Competence is your knowledge and skills. Consistency is your clarity and ability to be true to your word. Care encompasses your values as a leader and how those are demonstrated through action.'

These were the three pillars of credibility:

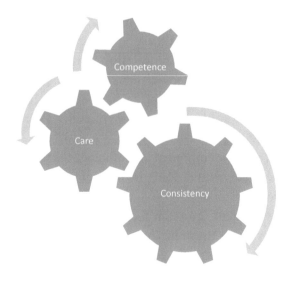

'While competence can gain you respect for what you're able to deliver and where you're able to guide the team, it is care and consistency that truly build credibility.'

Samanta recognized the truth of what he was saying. She thought of Jacob and how these principles applied to him. He had been incredibly competent and had earned the respect of his colleagues because of it. However, his ability to show care and be consistent needed some work. On some of the projects Samanta had worked on with Jacob, he had lost his temper often with the team and had badmouthed others behind their backs. Samanta remembered one such incident vividly.

They had just finished a presentation with a client and were flying back from the meeting. Jacob wasn't happy about how it had gone and felt that some of the client's questions were elementary. He started complaining about the client and saying how dumb he thought they were. Samanta was surprised. She wouldn't have expected such a reaction from a senior consultant. Client-centricity was a key focus for any leader at Pinnacle. Jacob was trampling upon the values of the firm in his tirade—and in front of junior consultants. He obviously wasn't aware of the effect his words were having, but Samanta was. She knew it was making a lasting impression on how the rest of the consultants perceived Jacob as a leader. Being a role model was central to being an effective leader.

With that incident in mind, she realized that the careful use of words and actions was critical in building a personal brand as a leader.

Executive Presence

Here's a lesson from thought leader and CEO coach Shital Kakkar Mehra, author of *Executive Presence: The P.O.I.S.E. Formula for Leadership*[3] and the business bestseller *Business Etiquette: A Guide for the Indian Professional*[4].

1.   What is the P.O.I.S.E. formula of executive presence?

Three years of research and interviews with more than 120 leaders across industries and functions have helped me come up with the proprietary P.O.I.S.E formula for executive presence:

---

[3]   S. Mehra, *Executive Presence: The P.O.I.S.E. Formula for Leadership*, HarperCollins, 2020.
[4]   S. Mehra, *Business Etiquette: A Guide for the Indian Professional,* HarperCollins, 2012.

- *Physical presence:* Refine your body language.
- *Online presence:* Build your global personal brand.
- *Influencer presence:* Master executive maturity; learn to 'speak up'.
- *Stage presence:* Inspire teams with effective public-speaking skills.
- *Engagement presence:* Build strong and diverse networks.

Each of these skills can be developed and can help one gain a competitive edge, leading to success in one's personal and professional life.

2. In your experience, is there any difference in how women and men see executive presence?

There are cultural and social factors to be considered to answer this question. Culturally, we have not trained women to be assertive in meetings. Also, in our culture, both men and women get emotional, which can work against us in our professional life.

3. What mistakes can hamper executive presence?

Each of us has a personal brand that is built over a number of years. It is important to work on it every day. Lack of accountability, not taking ownership of one's work, emotional outbursts, impulsive social media comments and poor relationship management inside and outside the organization can impact executive presence.

4. Is there any secret sauce to developing executive presence?

There is no secret sauce to building executive presence—it requires understanding its importance, taking stock of one's strengths and gaps in terms of key skills of executive presence, and working towards acquiring those skills. There are a few basics that can help.

- Clarity of thought.
- The ability to communicate in a clear and crisp manner.
- Body language (non-verbal communication) that conveys the presence of a winner.
- Strong online presence.
- Ability to influence stakeholders.
- Strong public-speaking skills.
- Managing remote teams.

5. Is business etiquette still relevant in modern workplaces, such as that of start-ups?

Yes, more so as rudeness has gone up in workplaces across the world. Today, work from home/remote working is the new trend, and it requires a strong presence—how one presents oneself on a video chat, for instance, can leave an impact, influence one's listeners.

A Man's World?

'Is this a man's world?' Samanta asked. Aekta stared back at her, wide-eyed. Samanta knew what she was thinking. A confident professional such as Samanta flying off the handle was unexpected. And it was the first time she had ever expressed this sentiment.

She had just finished a meeting with a group of leaders from a Japanese top-management team. The Pinnacle team led by Samanta was presenting a proposal. She was a principal consultant for them. She was annoyed by the fact that the group had placed more importance on the male members of her team. She had tried to interject a few times during the meeting but with no success. She felt discriminated against.

After recovering from her shock, Aekta listened patiently to Samanta.

'Sometimes,' Aekta said, 'male senior-management members from Japan can be a bit discriminating. They tend to be more patriarchal in their approach. You should make it clear to them that you're the right person for them to listen to and, if necessary, ask the men on your team to let you speak more often. Sometimes we have to push for our rightful space, and there's nothing wrong with that.'

Events such as these always left Samanta frustrated. Pinnacle was an equal-opportunity workplace. They nurtured talent—whether male or female. However, the ratio of women to men at Pinnacle, and in consulting in general, was lopsided. Many women would spend three or four years in consulting before switching to a non-consulting role or taking a break for family or other reasons. But Samanta was determined to make it big as a consultant. She knew it would be a struggle, but it would just be a matter of intelligent planning and hard work.

After Samanta became a manager, she had got married. It was a struggle to manage a highly demanding career and family responsibilities. Her husband, Abe, was an entrepreneur, and supportive of Samanta's career aspirations. Samanta knew that developing a healthy work-life balance would be key to getting her through the difficult years ahead. She knew it would be hard to excel in her consulting career without the rest of her life suffering. But she found that the more she tried to separate her work and personal life, the more tension it created.

It was Abe who helped her sort the issue out. He identified the guilt Samanta was feeling about not spending time with him or dedicating enough time to other personal areas of life. He understood that she needed to prioritize but still be flexible. Being a very structured person, Samanta always wanted control over every detail of her life, with a plan for everything. While this helped her stay disciplined, it often made her feel guilty when she was unable to adhere to her strict schedule. Abe, on the other hand, went with the flow. He advised her to minimize a few of the boundaries between work and the rest of her life. For example, he told her it was okay to take an urgent business call when they were having lunch together. Even weekends, when she was technically off work, would be full of clients needing help with one thing or another, making it impossible for her to keep it completely work-free. Abe told her it would be better to just set aside time during the weekend to deal with work-related issues, instead of trying to avoid them altogether and spending the weekend stressing about it.

An important revelation that Abe's advice helped bring to the surface was the realization that she kept thinking about things she needed to do for work during her time off, but didn't actually get any of it done. This form of keeping the two spheres of life separate wound up making things worse for her, since she spent the entire time worrying instead of getting things done and behind her.

'Abe, do you think it makes sense for me to take a sabbatical for a year for family reasons, and then come back to work afterwards?'

Abe was straightforward in his response. 'If you want to be successful in your career, you need to sort out this work–life issue. You can't be dreading your travel or late evenings all the time. I suggest you find a balance and flow that work for you. If you think a day is a bit light, don't try to fill it up. That's the perfect time to spend on hobbies, family or health.'

Samanta appreciated Abe's perspective. She always felt like Abe was more in control of his life than she was of hers. Though he ran a firm, he found time for her, his hobbies and sports, and even for his friends and extended family. She wondered if she found it more challenging because she was a woman.

She had a chat with Aekta about how she was feeling about this conflict between work, health, fun and family. She felt she spent too much time and focus on work, at the expense of other areas of her life—and no matter what she tried to focus on, she always felt the pressure to do something else, which made her constantly anxious. She wondered whether she would ever be able to find balance between the different areas of her life.

'Whatever choice you make, don't be guilty about it. Try to live with it and make the best of it,' Aekta said.

Samanta made some changes in her life after getting more tips on work-life integration from Abe and Aekta. She was happier and more satisfied with the changes after six months. She shared a few of her discoveries in a presentation during an annual retreat. This is what she said:

1. In work–life integration, there are no boundaries between weekdays and weekends. They overlap. It's all about balancing the work load. You may have to work on a Saturday evening and spend time with your family on a Tuesday morning. You do whatever is needed. You have to take control of the lean times in the week and make the

best use of them. Work this kind of flexibility out with your colleagues.

2. Whenever possible, try squeezing in activities you enjoy, including hobbies and health-related activities. For example, when you're travelling, visit a nearby place that you wanted to see or meet up with any friends you may have there. Use an extended weekend while travelling for work to enjoy a short vacation with family.

3. Watch what you eat. Even while travelling or meeting clients, try to eat as healthy as possible.

4. Enjoy travelling and don't treat it as a chore. See it as an opportunity to meet new people and, occasionally, new places. You could minimize the dreadful feeling of packing bags every Sunday and start doing it with much more ease of mind after changing your perspective.

5. Sometimes discussing work with a spouse or other family members also helps. They try to give you a more neutral perspective on what's happening. While some people may work hard to keep work and life conversations separate, work–life integration can actually mean that they supplement each other. You can also be more open about family and life at work as well. This can help your seniors and team members better understand your needs.

'You're always cogitating about something! What are you brooding about this time?'

Samanta was surprised at Raghav's outburst. Samanta and Raghav hadn't worked together this closely on a project since their intern days years earlier. Raghav had become an expert in digital transformation, and even more than his expertise in that field, his language skills had become legendary. Every now and then, he would pull out a few odd words here and there, just so he could laugh at the strange look on the unfortunate recipient's face. Samanta didn't disappoint.

'Am I a cow ruminating now?' she shot back.

He smiled. 'It's just that you always look preoccupied. Sometimes, it's important to clear your mind.'

She frowned. She knew he was speaking sense, especially at this point in her life. She couldn't stop thinking about work. It was like having her switch flipped on 24x7. She knew that while there was work–life integration, just thinking about work instead of doing something about it was a waste of time and simply added stress to her life. As they worked together on the project, Raghav pointing out when she was lost in her thoughts helped her refocus and stop stressing.

Be the Catalyst or the Change Agent

A consultant is a catalyst for change, a role Samanta was passionate about. At the end of the day, she knew her objective was to help the client be more effective. The underlying belief of the profession was that there was always room for improvement, and a consultant was entrusted with guiding the client through that process. It was similar to a patient–doctor relationship. Sometimes, the patient knows what the problem is, but it's the doctor that helps them discover the root cause and understand how to treat it.

Samanta's training during her MBA taught her about the frameworks, models and tools needed to affect change at an individual, team and organizational level. As she worked with businesses to help them thrive, many interesting models came to mind from her past training.

Samanta was part of a project aimed at radically reducing expenditures in a large private bank in the Middle East. It was a challenging project, as the Middle Eastern economy was in a constant growth phase and the top management seldom thought about cost. On the other hand, the project was also interesting, because it required a total change in mindset on the part of the organization. The potential cost savings the Pinnacle team envisaged was in the range of $50 million over a two-year period. Apart from the fixed fees, Pinnacle's fees were tied to the actual achieved savings on each of the cost items. The first step of the project required identifying each area of expenditure and then drawing up a plan to cut those costs without affecting business growth or operations. The main goal was to minimize costs and leverage technology so the company could become truly profitable.

A wide range of expertise in different areas was needed to complete the project. Areas such as finance and budgeting, processes and manpower optimization. Samanta and her team took the time to address each of these areas and thoroughly analyse the various costs. After completing this step of the process, the next step was to convince the management team to adopt a 'zero-based budgeting' approach. In the past, the company had taken an incremental approach to budgeting, changing the budget by slight degrees to meet the requirements of the year. They would make the changes with no questions asked, often ignoring existing budgeted costs. This way of handling the budget had to stop.

Samanta found that, often, performing an effective analysis wasn't the most challenging part of these projects. Obtaining buy-in from the leadership and impressing upon them the urgent need for change was. To minimize this issue, Samanta and her team worked closely with a core group of the company's leadership, including the CEO. Together, they led workshops involving the rest of the department teams to go over the various cost elements, assessing the relevance of the cost to the success of the company. The goal was not to reduce core operating costs but to cut back on discretionary costs that did little to advance the company's interests. The Pinnacle team also worked to refine various processes for greater efficiency. This included procurement streamlining, optimizing marketing initiatives and vendor renegotiations.

During this process, the top consultants in the Pinnacle team, including Samanta, recognized the need to help the stakeholders own the change for themselves. One way they did this was to have a member of the leadership team kick off every workshop dealing with cost optimization with a brief on the urgent need to follow the new path they had charted. The leadership team also put the rest of the team members at ease by assuring them they wouldn't lose their jobs but that they needed to make changes to the way their daily tasks were performed to increase the business's effectiveness. Buy-in from the team was encouraged by giving each member the freedom to express their opinions during the workshops.

At the start of the project, the leadership and Pinnacle team had decided on a 25 per cent cost-reduction goal. By the end of the process, many of the teams had hit the target goal but others had not. If the team had valid reasons for the cost, the consulting team didn't push them too hard. The situation brought Kurt Lewin's force field analysis and his three-step model on change to Samanta's mind. The force field analysis identified the forces assisting change and the forces hampering it. For example, in the case of the cost transformation, the forces were broken down as:

Forces for	Forces against
Poor profitability that could impact overall company existence	Fear of job loss
Cash-flow challenges	Fear of looking bad in front of management due to questioning by consultants
The CEO's goals for profitability	Loss of control over budget and discretionary spending
Possible induction of better processes	Fear of losing key projects due to tightened control
Enhancing procurement— better vendors and better quality, leading to better prices	Loss of employee perks
Possible incentives and performance pay due to better performance	Increased effort requirements for process changes and new ways of working

It was important that the workshops address the fears the team members were dealing with, along with accelerate the progress towards change. Overall, Samanta was pleased with the way her team had applied the principles of effective change as outlined by John Kotter, professor, author and an expert in change management. The principles were broadly:

Create a sense of urgency	The client CEO communicated the imminent profitability challenges that could lead to job losses if costs were not contained. Also, the need to proceed with fiscal prudence due to poor market conditions was highlighted.
Form a powerful guiding coalition	A core group of top leaders was formed. Multiple leaders communicated the need for change to the various stakeholders.
Create a vision	The vision of a transformed organization and plans to transform it were articulated. The CEO spoke about a more profitable and efficient organization as part of the cost transformation, as well as highlighted the need for wasteful spending to be identified and reduced. Also, he presented plans for making the processes more efficient for employee productivity.
Communicate the vision	Townhalls, small group meetings and other communication on the 'how' and 'why' of the change process were intentionally initiated.
Empower others to act on the vision	Each business head and their leaders were given freedom to take the final decision. The consultants asked incisive questions to aid the process.

Plan for and create short-term wins	The zero-based budgeting process in one of the units alone saved 30 per cent of the costs. The consulting team used this to create momentum for the overall cost reduction process.
Consolidate improvements and produce still more changes	The wins in the formation of better processes and in each of the business units helped build more momentum. Employees were also given the opportunity to share ideas on how to improve productivity and reduce costs.
Institutionalize new changes	The managers and key stakeholders were trained in the new processes. The dos and don'ts for cost management were shared. The CEO and his team led by example. Changes in structure were incorporated, which required any large expenditure to be approved by a top-level committee, irrespective of the expenditure being budgeted. This enabled the organization to review the strategic relevance of the expense at a future date.

One of the other frameworks on change management taught to consultants at Pinnacle was the 'Change Commitment Curve'. This framework helped a consultant understand the phases of change and what effect it had on the employees at various stages of change. The framework, developed by

Daryl Conner and Robert Patterson, envisioned seven progressive levels of commitment to change. These are multiple stages of change and, in the framework, it is broadly classified as 'Inform', 'Educate' and 'Commit'.

Inform

1. *Contact:* Employees getting to know of the change that is going to be effected.
2. *Awareness:* Awareness of the scope of the change.
3. *Understanding:* Understanding the impact on the organization, function and self.

Educate

4. *Positive perception:* A perception of the positive impact of the change.
5. *Adoption:* Individuals willing to work towards the change.
6. *Embedding change:* Sustaining the new way of working.

Commit

7. *Internalization:* Employees internalizing and starting to improvise on the change and increasing its effectiveness.

At any of these stages, the change effort can fall apart and the momentum of change may not happen. In a consulting assignment, sometimes, Pinnacle only provided the strategy and did not get involved in the active implementation. In the case of this bank, Pinnacle had to get results to make the project successful. A lot of effort was put into communication and education on the new ways of doing things.

However, despite the consulting team's best efforts, the project wasn't completely smooth. One of the business heads was particularly sceptical of the initiative. The business was doing well, and he felt that taking extra time to focus on cost management wasn't worth it. Samanta found that there were always people opposed to the changes, and this project was no exception. In this case, the CEO met the leader in private to ensure his fears were addressed. The CEO was able to show the leader the future implications of not being part of the process. Samanta knew it was sometimes necessary to manoeuvre change process by taking help from a few key stakeholders.

In a different project, there was another problem related to effecting positive change that Samanta had to face. The key elements of effecting positive change are the credibility of the leader sponsoring the change and the process that is followed throughout. If the leader lacks credibility, the chance of change goes down drastically. The same problem occurs when the process he or she is following is questionable. This is what happened in the project, where Samanta was working with a large financial services team that was midway through a transformation process. The CEO started making claims about the changes that were being made, and acting like they were already a reality, even though most of them were still in process. From his point of view, it was harmless, since the changes were on the way, but it created a lot of disillusionment within the organization. The credibility of the CEO, and even Pinnacle, was brought into question. The employees became suspicious of the top management and the consultants after that.

Something Samanta did very well as a consultant was remove ambiguity with logic. She liked to be certain when there was uncertainty. Like most consultants, she was a change agent for her clients. In this role, it was important for her to work with everyone involved in the change process—from the executive team to the implementers themselves. It was easy to give recommendations on a large scale, but organizations wanted and needed the changes to happen on the ground. This was challenging, since the members of the executive team leading the charge were often busy in their other roles, requiring the consultant to keep the momentum going, or the change might not happen at all. She had learnt about the Chaos Theory by Tom Peters. It meant that any company that was able to respond to the changes and the chaos in the environment was generally more successful. This called for organizations to be responsive and have a plan for change—however small it was.

This made a change agent an adept educator. It was their job to equip the various stakeholders in successfully completing the change process. For example, in a project involving a zero-based budgeting process, Samanta had to present the process to multiple teams, including finance and accounting. Since financial experts in the accounting team were involved, Samanta's role was to help them realize they needed to adjust their wording to match the way the sponsor and the consultant were presenting the process to the other employees, so the message was clear.

In her experience, this kind of communication of the change process worked best when the following three factors were kept in mind:

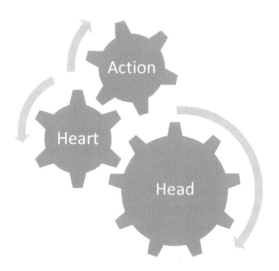

The head is the logic of the process crafted by the sponsor and the consultant. The logic needs to be relevant to the various stakeholders for it to make sense to them.

The heart denotes how much the logic and appeal from the sponsor is able to make an emotional impact on the rest of the team. As a consultant, when one is communicating or having a dialogue, it is important that one not miss the emotions and perceptions that people carry about the change. It is important that the consultant is able to sense and allay the fears that they may have as much as possible. As an experienced consultant, one of the aspects Samanta saw was the eagerness of many junior consultants to analyse and rationalize these fears, and tendency to be sarcastic about the 'silliness' of the reasons behind the fears. With experience, Samanta realized that it was important to empathize with the concerns and provide solutions that would help win their hearts.

Action is the series of efforts taken by the various stakeholders to make the change happen.

Whenever the chance arose, Samanta stressed that the full alignment of the organization was required for change to happen. For example, if cost management was an area of focus, she stressed that performance-management systems be aligned with them, and that MIS (Management Information System/Reporting) track the cost-related variables, which be then reported and discussed.

The worst-case scenario in any change-management process involves a change in the sponsor. A change in the CEO, or even a key stakeholder, can cause enormous turmoil. An example of this occurred in a project focused on growth strategy, for which Samanta was the project manager. The regional director, who was the key stakeholder, was all for an expansion into African countries. He had a good grasp of the market and worked in close partnership with the consultants. However, midway through the project, a new stakeholder took charge. He was an outsider and a former consultant. The new vice president of strategic initiatives had his own viewpoint and started questioning everything about the project.

Samanta knew that buy-in from this new vice president was critical if the project was to succeed. Instead of defending what they had accomplished so far, she updated him on their progress and asked for his input. She knew it was important that he take ownership of the project. Samanta also started incorporating ideas from him that she thought were useful. A key skill Samanta used in such situations was to be neutral and open to change, so long as it didn't destroy the core of the project.

In an interesting study by BCG on change management, the authors[5] looked at change from a 'biological' management process. This stressed on adaptive change management and looked at changing methods and the process of change based on what was working. Impact assessment was done and the course corrections were incorporated to make it work. A good consultant should be able to guide and support the client through this process. The use of technology and digital transformation can help bring out the desired changes. Technology can be a supportive tool—for example, the use of digital games for communication, or the change itself can be the digital transformation. The use of technology was changing the processes and how organizations could be more effective. The question that always remains is whether employees are ready to embrace them.

What Keeps Individuals from Changing?

'If you keep doing what you are doing, you will keep getting what you are getting'

—Anonymous

At the heart of it, individuals do not like much change as it means moving out of their comfort zones. As teams and organizations are also a sum of individuals, the same logic can be applied to them as well. Many times, a consultant is

---

5   L. Faeste, M. Reeves and K. Whitaker, 'The Science of Organizational Change', BCG Henderson Institute, 2019, https://www.bcg.com/en-sea/publications/2019/science-organizational-change.aspx (accessed on 5 January 2021).

brought in to ensure that the need and process of change are well ingrained in the system.

One of Samanta's favourite frameworks to explain the need for change on a personal level was the 'Johari Window'. The Johari Window acted as a mirror to show individuals their awareness levels and where they needed to change. The Johari Window is given below:

Open Area: Known to self and others	Blind Spot: Not known to self but known to others
Hidden Area: Known to self but not known to others	Unknown: Not known to self or others

Developed by two psychologists, Joseph Luft and Harrington Ingham,[6] the Johari Window provides an intuitive way of looking at awareness and change in an individual. Most of the senior leaders Samanta worked with as a consultant had blind spots they developed over the years. As one grew in the organization, it was difficult to receive relevant input, and peers and junior colleagues were often reluctant to share their feedback.

Leadership development is an important element in any transformation project. Structure and process changes may occur, but, in most cases, the core of the change relates to the level of engagement and development among the leadership.

The most common areas to address in any transformation project are strategy, structure, processes and people. Changes in the other areas are driven by the people involved, making

---

6   J. Luft and H. Ingham, 'The Johari Window: A Graphic Model of Interpersonal Awareness', *Proceedings of the Western Training Laboratory in Group Development*, Los Angeles.

this the most critical area on which to focus, with leadership taking the bulk of that focus.

Samanta remembered working with a non-banking financial organization that wanted to double its turnover in the next three years. A private equity partner had major investments in the firm and was expecting exponential growth to take place in the company. The main issues clearly involved geographic expansion and product innovation, which were tackled in the proposed strategy. However, the 'people' element wasn't addressed, causing their carefully laid-out plan to grind to a halt and requiring them to create a new initiative focused exclusively on developing their people.

Crafting a talent strategy turned out to be one of the most interesting parts of the assignment. Samanta and her team came up with a plan to attract, develop and retain the talent required for the growth strategy to move forward smoothly. The structural elements were already in place, but having the people to compliment that structure was key. They settled on the idea of developing a hundred leaders within the organization who would be the main force driving the new growth plan. This part of the project was titled '100 CEOs'. They would be trained and equipped to take on the next level of business roles.

Pinnacle conducted an assessment of the current leadership teams to better understand how to move forward. The assessment included tools such as assessment centres, psychometric instruments and a 360-degree assessment plan. They compiled the strengths and weaknesses of the leadership teams into the following:

Strengths	Weaknesses
High result focus	Lack of innovative mindset
Driven and self-motivated	Poor at change management and working in ambiguity
Customer-centric	Weak in talent development
Process-oriented	Averse to risk-taking
Good at driving performance	Minimal strategic orientation

The analysis showed that though they were managing well for then, they weren't developing the leadership necessary to prepare for the future and the challenges the company would inevitably face. The capabilities they possessed weren't enough to help the organization reinvent itself and align to the new change strategy.

The next step after understanding the talent landscape was to select the best strategy for developing the needed capabilities in the leadership.

Samanta had an interesting conversation with Robin, a leadership coach who worked in leadership change. He was an interesting personality. He had been the CEO of a large organization before deciding to leave his corporate career and pursue business coaching. Samanta had always been curious about leadership change and wanted to gain insight from Robin, especially during this massive change process. She reached out to him and they met over coffee to talk.

'How is it that leaders get stuck when it comes to their own development?' Samanta said, thinking about the leaders they were working with and how many of them had stagnated in their personal growth.

Robin chuckled. 'How many of us genuinely like feedback?'

She smiled. 'You have a point there.'

He leaned back in his chair and looked at the ceiling. 'As we become more senior and successful in our careers, we love to hear positive feedback about how we're doing. As a result of our position and experience, the opportunities to get genuine feedback diminish. I mean, who actually wants to say the emperor is naked?'

Samanta nodded. 'Then how do you make a leader realize their need for change?' she asked.

'Assessments by the organization or consultants provide the leaders with a feedback report. That can be a good starting point. In many cases, there could be obvious performance or behavioural issues that need to be dealt with. It's always important for the leaders to be shown their blind spots.' He took a sip of his coffee before shrugging and continuing. 'Some leaders take it well. Others try to justify themselves. When I'm coaching, my job is to show them evidence to back up my observations, share relevant feedback and get them to reflect. I would say probably 60–70 per cent eventually recognize the areas they need to develop.'

'So how does coaching work?'

'Ah, good question. I've been working recently with the CEO of a large company. He's well respected in the industry. He's received feedback from his team members that he is very task-focused and doesn't relate to the people around him on a personal level. As a result, there's very little emotional engagement with the team. The CEO wanted to see this change, and came to me. I use the "GROW" model of coaching, which stands for "Goals", what you want to achieve; "Reality", what the current reality is; "Options", for what can be done; and "Will", what one can do. The CEO wanted to connect emotionally with the team and build engagement. So that was his goal as we went through the coaching process. Next, he listed the current reality. Most of his interactions with the team were transactional and task-oriented. He treated them as subordinates, even though they were senior leaders. I asked him what he was willing to do to change the situation, and we came up with a plan for him to work on.

'He took the time to follow the steps we charted out, which wasn't easy. He got to know the team members personally, he put in the effort to become familiar with their challenges at work and, instead of telling, he took the time to ask meaningful questions. He also shared a lot more about himself with his colleagues. At the end of six months, there was visible change in the relationship between the CEO and the team. The CEO shared with me the changes he was implementing and their impact. My job was to listen and make suggestions that I felt were relevant.'

Samanta nodded as she followed what Robin was saying. This was very interesting.

'What do you think makes coaching work?'

'I would say it boils down to three factors. First, the chemistry between the coach and coachee. Second, the coachee's willingness to take feedback and suggestions. And third, the coachee's eagerness to change. No amount of coaching will help if the one being coached isn't willing to change.'

Samanta found the information helpful. It cleared up many questions she had about coaching, and she knew it would be valuable as she and her team moved forward with the change project.

Pinnacle facilitated many interventions to help the change happen. Each was aligned to the leadership competencies the organization wanted to match its strategy to. The interventions helped enhance the knowledge, skills and attitudes related to each desired competency. For example, if innovation was an area that needed to be developed by a leader, the underlying issues could include limited knowledge of the concepts and processes of innovation (knowledge), an inability to put the knowledge into action (skills) or a mindset that hindered the competency from being developed (attitude). Knowledge could be acquired through reading, attending workshops or learning from others. Skills could be developed through practice. Attitudes were often the most challenging. They could stem from something as simple as thoughts such as 'this content isn't relevant', 'the organization's values are misplaced' or 'there are too many things on my plate'. In most cases, it was the attitudes and core mindsets that drove behaviour. The comprehensive development programme Pinnacle created was designed to support the key people most equipped to promote individual leadership change.

Samanta was talking to the senior partner, KK, when he made this pronouncement. 'Individuals don't like change. Change takes effort and often makes us confront our own assumptions.'

She had to agree with him there.

He went on to demonstrate his point. 'I was working with an organization's head of sales a while back, who was known to have lavish parties for his immediate team. He thought people loved him because of his extravagance but received sobering feedback when promotion time rolled around. He was told he needed to change his leadership style based on his team's feedback that he was overly aggressive, was constantly driven to win and often used abusive language at work. It was a rude awakening for him. He felt cheated by his team, whom he had thought he took good care of.'

Samanta nodded. She'd seen similar things herself.

KK shrugged. 'Often, leaders are in denial and try to justify the feedback they receive. It's important that the person coaching them help them reflect on their behaviours. Change is gradual, and often starts with minor changes in behaviour. These changes in behaviour do need to be consistent, however. The leader needs to be aware of his or her reactions to each new situation and be careful not to fall back into old behaviour patterns.'

KK mentioned the concept of 'cultivated learning' to Samanta once. 'Learning is an art that needs to be refined by each learner,' KK reflected. 'As one grows in one's career, there are new areas that one needs to learn—and also unlearn. Just like a tree is cultivated, this learning should be a planned process by the individual. '

KK spoke about three aspects of cultivated learning— purpose, passion and skills. Cultivated learning brought the desired skills and passion in place to ensure the purpose was fulfilled.

6

The Networker

Samanta had some interesting discussions with KK. He was the most connected senior partner she had ever worked with at Pinnacle. While she learnt something every time they talked, she always wondered at his networking skills.

'It took me decades to build the connections I have,' KK told her. 'It was definitely the Pinnacle brand that opened doors for me but the relationships were built through my own efforts.'

He shared more on how to build lasting connections during a large client conference, where he shared his insights. As he shared, Samanta could tell that he was completely relaxed as he shared confidently and naturally to a room full of top executives. He spoke to them as equals, sharing genuine connections with them and speaking more about them and their lives. During the event, it was quite common for Samanta to observe executives connecting KK with others. In a matter of hours, he had built more than two dozen new relationships. The most interesting part was that he introduced Samanta to each of the people he had just met, while still meeting new people himself. He introduced her as a competent consultant who was doing interesting work in a number of areas. Sometimes, he left her to have a longer conversation with some of the new connections. Those often ended with potential meeting opportunities or invitations from some of them to present her work to the top leadership at their respective firms.

While having a chat with KK after the event, Samanta asked him the secret to building relationships. He drew a figure showing the 4 Cs of networking.

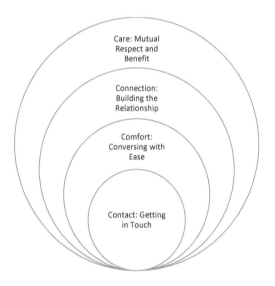

'Many of our connections don't go beyond the stage of getting in touch,' KK said. 'It might be just an initial introduction, and many of us consultants forget about it immediately after. From "contact" to "comfort" is a matter of navigating a conversation in such a way that the other person feels at ease conversing with you. There are four kinds of people you'll encounter at this stage.' He went on to describe them:

The Openers	They are open for a quick conversation. If they find you interesting, they may spend a little more time.
The Wheelers	They may spend a few moments with you, but are not really interested in building new relationships.
The Builders	Builders are there for new contacts and to build genuine connections. They believe that each person has something unique to offer.
The Blockers	Very difficult to reach out to and often block access to their work or personal life unless they feel you are connected to their inner circle.

To connect with each kind of networker is an important skill that a consultant should master. Samanta remembered an early consulting assignment where she had worked with the promoters of a family brand.

Samanta was thinking about her own experience while listening to KK. Alan, a client of Samanta, who was one of the promoter family members, was a typical blocker. She remembered that he constantly had a wall up. He seldom made casual conversation, preferring to keep the topics business-centric. The only person who had been able to build a relationship with him was Hamid. Hamid had broken into the inner circle by sharing comprehensive knowledge about the industry, and managed to engage him by delving further into business topics.

KK continued, 'It takes a while for blockers to trust others but they are willing to invest time in getting to know someone if they find the interaction and subsequent relationship relevant. Also, once a relationship is built with a blocker, it can last a long time.

'Builders are curious about what you do, who you are and what you can offer. They put in time and effort to build relationships and expect the same treatment in return. To connect with builders, be prepared to put in the time and effort necessary to get to know them. This often looks like having long conversations without an agenda. Be aware that they are judging you throughout this process to assess what you have to bring to the table. They usually enjoy long dinners and prefer to discuss a wide range of topics in informal conversation. They believe that relationships are personal and that building connections should precede purpose.

'Wheelers don't share the same need for a deep connection. They're usually just there to enjoy the moment, and getting much engagement from them is difficult. It is also difficult to establish rapport or a deep relationship with them. The hard part is that they often seem like builders at first but don't follow up after you part ways.

'Openers are better than wheelers. They do a quick assessment of you, and typically move away after a cordial conversation. They appear interested, but if you don't capture their interest with an elevator speech right away, it's rare for them to engage with you for long thereafter.'

'In my experience, many business leaders tend to become openers or blockers over a period of time. But a good consultant is able to break through their walls and reach their hearts and minds.' Samanta was happy after the discussion with KK. 'I think I got a lot out of this conversation,' she reflected.

Samanta was eager to build her network, and the fact that she was an extrovert didn't hurt. She knew that having a solid network was critical to business and career success. While many, such as KK, showed her the ropes, she knew the skill could only be honed through experience.

Samanta's stint in Singapore as part of a special assignment proved to contain her most interesting experience in networking. She was building a new business from the ground up in a new business environment. Her network in Singapore to that point only included a few colleagues from Pinnacle and some business contacts she had acquired during regional assignments. She could probably count all of them on her fingers.

KK had once told her, 'Networking is an art, but network-building is a strategy.' She wanted to have a clear strategy for building a strong network among decision-makers and influencers within the Singapore business community—and all within a year. She took a three-pronged approach to create a funnel she had in mind:

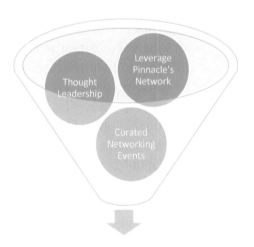

Potential Business Contacts

Samanta met every partner and senior consultant at Pinnacle in person after joining the Singapore office. This move helped her build her internal network. Since Samanta's practice was relatively new, many of the senior leaders at Pinnacle were ready to connect her with their clients. She made it a point to schedule follow-up meetings and presentations with each of the clients as soon as she had finished the initial introductions with them. One key thing Samanta learnt was that educating people was the best way to connect with them. The moment someone felt they were receiving new ideas or learning something from Samanta's discussions and presentations, they felt obliged to build a relationship.

The area of thought leadership helped in brand-building and establishing oneself as an expert in the field. During the period of building the practice, Samanta committed to working on thought leadership with the goal of being seen as a frontrunner in the field. She pored over global studies Pinnacle had conducted so she could gain more knowledge of the field. The work she had done in market-entry strategies, and in building the analytics practice, had given her a lot of material to share with others. Presenting at industry forums and writing about the topic in industry journals helped her spread her knowledge—and, of course, her name.

She also tried something interesting. She interviewed twenty key stakeholders on the topic of 'the state of analytics adoption' in their companies. The process helped her share best practices and learn about the gaps the company might want to fill in that area.

Networking events were common in Singapore. Since she had started being recognized more and more as a thought leader, she was able to participate in many events as a key speaker, sharing new material from her vast stores of knowledge. The events were attended by a curated list of business leaders, which helped Samanta spend time with relevant people. These networking events also helped her strategically position her personal brand and practice to gain more attention in the market.

She gained many valuable connections during that time and felt she could connect with most of the relevant leaders on a business level. However, the challenge now was to move to the level of 'care'—mutual respect and benefit.

'I am always comfortable discussing business and ideas,' she shared with KK. 'But I'm uneasy when it comes to relationships and informal conversations.'

KK raised his eyebrows and chuckled. 'I have to say I'm a little surprised. You're one of the most confident women I know.' He paused for a moment. 'That reminds me of an article I read in the *Harvard Business Review*.[1] The topic was the secrets of successful female networkers, and was based on the research of Inga Carboni and others who interviewed more than 16,500 men and women over half a decade. They discovered four characteristics of successful female networkers.'

He went on to explain them:

Efficient	Successful networkers are focused on time management. They identify and say 'no' to both work that doesn't add value and to time spent on unnecessary operational activities. They are perceived more as 'strategic and thoughtful'. Others tend to have a positive outlook on associating with them.
Nimble	While long-lasting relationships are important to build and maintain, some efficient networkers prioritize 'new' connections over the 'old' ones. While this can be seen as opportunistic, it can also be seen as professional and more work-oriented.

[1] 'The Secrets of Successful Female Networkers', *Harvard Business Review*, November–December 2019, Vol. 97, Issue 6, pp.19–23.

Boundary Spanning	Boundary-spanning is the openness to and the effort taken to have a wide range of relationships, even beyond one's natural areas of expertise or comfort level. It's about constantly evaluating each potential connection and seeking ways to connect when possible.
Energy-Balanced	The research by the authors provides an interesting perspective on how female professionals can use their strengths in the networking process. Successful female networkers use a mix of competence, warmth, intelligence and emotional intelligence while networking, which helps them build trust faster and have better relationships.

'I think I'm good at the first three,' Samanta said, tapping her chin. 'I'm not sure about the fourth.' She knew she was competent and intelligent, but the challenge arose when she tried to bring the human element into the mix. She felt she came across as too businesslike when building connections.

'Here's a helpful way to think about it,' said KK. 'Most CEOs and business leaders are like you and me. Do your best to visualize them that way. You'll be more confident if you talk to them with that imagery in mind. You've heard of ego states. It's important that you have the conversations as one adult to another. Don't fall into the "adapted child" ego state and cringe when you see a senior business leader, whether male or female.' He gestured to indicate the two of them. 'Try to have a conversation just like you and I are having, or like you'd have with a colleague or someone you know well. Keep it interesting and engaging. As a consultant from Pinnacle, they are going to ask you all the time what new things are happening. You just need to build on that. You have to speak up and get a conversation going. Nobody can stop you.'

Ego States

Eric Berne, a renowned psychiatrist from Canada, conceptualized and popularized transactional analysis to the world through his seminal book *Games People Play*.[2] Transactional analysis describes how the personalities of people are structured psychologically based on their ego states. The three ego states described by Berne are 'parent', 'adult' and 'child'. The basic interactions of people are wired based on their scripted personality aligned to these ego states.

- *Parent*: The parent ego state has two ways of expressing—being nurturing and being critical. A nurturing individual would be transacting along the lines of 'from my experience, it would help you best in your career if you are able to develop your listening skills', while a critical parent ego state would be something like, 'If you do not listen to others, you will not have a future in this job.' The behaviours are driven by how they would be unconsciously reflecting their parents' behaviours/other influential people's behaviours in similar situations. The nurturing parent ego state comes from a feeling of supporting and developing while the critical parent is driven by authority and discipline.
- *Adult*: When a person is in the adult ego state, the individual is at the rational best. In this ego state, the person sees the current reality, has a more unbiased approach and can take decisions. In this state, the

---

[2] Eric Berne, *Games People Play: The Psychology of Human Relationships*, Penguin UK, 1968.

individual has his/her logic and reasoning at their best. The mind is programmed to take decisions based on the best available information.

- *Child*: In this ego state, the individual, just like a child, is the source of creation, joy, emotion, love, care and playfulness, and is rebellious and unreasonable. The child ego state can manifest in two different ways—the natural child, which is full of curiosity, creativity, naïvete and emotions; and an adapted child, which has changed or modified to the environment through interactions or needs. These include being overaggressive, rebellious, resisting, indisciplined and conforming.

It is interesting to analyse how an ideal leader would behave when seen through the lens of these ego states. In a traditional outlook, the leader is mostly seen as a mix of nurturing parent, critical parent, adult and a natural child. This would mean that the leader is able to guide and support the team, discipline and draw boundaries, take decisions based on data and reality, and also bring the emotions, fun, life and creativity to work. However, based on the context, including the type of organization and the type of the team that the leader has, different ego states might work best. For example, in a highly creative organization, the leader can be in a natural child ego state, and the creativity, fun and joyfulness that the leader brings can help bring the team together. Similarly, in a highly hierarchical, paternalistic culture, the leader who can balance the parent and adult ego states may be the best bet as a leader.

Extending the idea of ego states proposed by Berne, Thomas A. Harris, the author of the book *I'm OK–You're OK*,[3] explained how the transactions between individuals operating from the different ego states will pan out. People might take overall four life positions that can influence their behaviour. These are 'I'm OK–You're OK', 'I'm OK–You're Not OK', 'I'm Not OK–You're OK' and 'I'm Not OK–You're Not OK'. These life positions are dependent on the dominant ego state that influences thought and behaviour. In a leadership position, taking a paternalistic ego state and operating from a mindset of 'I'm OK–You're Not OK' may lead to disengagement and conflict with team members, who might not be in an ego state of child to accept the parent ego state the leader is in. In another popular book, *Born to Win*,[4] authors Muriel James and Dorothy Jongeward stress the importance of understanding that leadership effectiveness is often a reflection of the leader's ability to understand that each discussion is a transaction and there are ego states involved in it. Often, behaviour changes that are expected in executive coaching for leaders involve delving to the basic drivers motivated through the ego states and the life positions. The overemphasis and dominance of certain ego states and life positions can lead to dysfunctional leadership behaviours, often leading to narcissism, being taken lightly, the inability to see reality, blame games and often refusing to change.

---

[3]   T.A. Harris, *I'm OK–You're OK*, Random House, 2012.

[4]   M. James and D. Jongeward, *Born to Win: Transactional Analysis with Gestalt Experiments*, Addison-Wesley, 1971, pp. 64–65.

Samanta smiled at KK's words. He had delivered the last part like a motivational speaker.

Apart from external networking, internal networking was also important. Samanta made it a point to connect with and learn from as many senior leaders in the company as she could.

Samanta also set out to break the assumptions some people had about female consultants. She didn't shy away from consulting engagements that required her to work in traditional or male-oriented industries. She also took on assignments typically avoided by other women in the firm such as heavy engineering.

Samanta's three principles of building her network were:

Thought leadership	Connecting based on knowledge and the expertise one has to offer. Sharing blogs and articles related to one's area of expertise through various media outlets is also included in this principle.
Being non-transactional	Connections are not for immediate benefit. It's important the connections are made as 'humans' and not transactions.
Connecting as equals	Making sure there is mutual respect and trust when making connections. While there is positional hierarchy within the network, it's important that it not stop one from sharing one's viewpoints and opinions.

Pinnacle gave extensive training on how to conduct oneself. Observing some of the best consultants and senior executives in the company helped Samanta define how she conducted herself within the firm and outside. It was a process of learning for her—something that was defined as 'executive presence'. In one of her interactions with the managing partner of the firm, the gentleman said, 'We are a modern, diverse, sophisticated, cutting-edge and competitive organization. We value talent that drives these characteristics.' This was an interesting way to define the organization and kind of people they preferred to have in the firm. It was definitely how Pinnacle worked—with talented people who were sophisticated, articulate, highly knowledgeable and competitive. That was the 'talent culture' of Pinnacle. There was space only for people who were constant learners and high on initiative. It was also important to be competitive while being collaborative. A tough ask when one was surrounded by folks who were very driven.

It was Aekta who provided some really valuable insights into building executive presence. It was a client presentation and the vice president of the finance division asked a question that seemed to undermine the credibility of the recommendations. Samanta was taken aback by the tone of the question and was not sure whether her response would be the right one. She seemed unsure of what she was saying. She also said they would check on it and come back. After the meeting, Aekta was not very happy with Samanta's handling of the question. 'We have reviewed this aspect multiple times and you had the right answer. Why were you so hesitant? Let me tell you, Samanta, if you want to be seen as a credible consultant, be confident in your responses. You are the person in the room who knows the data best! Your tone, your posture and facial expressions all communicate that confidence. Get it right.'

Samanta also observed how one could make subtle changes to how one conducted oneself depending on the client situation. While there were standards of how a Pinnacle consultant should conduct himself/herself, different clients had different contexts and cultures. The seriousness in the room, the formality, the language used, and the expressed hierarchy, could all be different. She had seen how Aekta and other senior partners could easily align themselves to the 'sense of the room' and present themselves accordingly. In some meetings, the participants just wanted to hear you speak; in some they wanted democratic debates; a few were leaderless; and some were autocratic. A high sensing helped one align with the crowd in the room.

The Relationship Builder: Riaz Hassen, managing partner, Colombo Leadership Academy, Sri Lanka

1. As the CEO of Colombo Leadership Academy, you have built great relationships with key stakeholders. What are your principles of relationship-building?

The key to building professional relationships that improve your presence is well-planned networking, and participating in talk shows, debates, forums and workshops. However, a good leader can articulate his/her own relationship-building through leveraging the contacts already made through further interactions on inviting them to participate in open programmes, awareness-building sessions and forums, and increasing the interactions to a point where they appreciate their involvement.

   In consulting, it is all about professional involvement. I seek to build relationships as an adviser, an expert and a provider of solutions they value. We invest time and effort to conduct presentations/workshops with the top management to share some of the work that we do. Many of these interactions help us connect at a professional and personal level. It is also important to be in constant touch and update the network about what is happening at one's professional front.

I also leverage social media to build the company's brand, along with my personal brand. This also helps create better recall with the clients.

2. How do you handle conflict when it comes to clients?

Conflicts are opportunities and a test to validate leadership agility, whether the leader is continuously learning from good and bad outcomes. The learnings from conflict are important so that our performance improves and develops our standard of leadership to prevent conflicts. Whenever there is conflict, the leaders must learn to view it from a vantage point. Instead of dealing with a problem in isolation, we take a holistic look and make sure such conflicts are avoided in future.

3. How do you sense the organizational ecosystem and its culture when you start an engagement with a new client?

Each of our clients has a unique way of working. The leadership styles, decision-making process, communication flow and values are different. As a consultant, you need to observe and be aware of them. Appreciating them and also making them feel you respect their ways of working is important to gain trust and credibility.

7

Management Consulting Tools

Over the years Samanta spent at Pinnacle, she used multiple management tools and practices to help her build structure and solve client problems. Some of these tools and practices are well known and have stood the test of time. A few of these include:

SWOT Analysis

When new clients come up with a problem, consultants often conduct a SWOT analysis. A SWOT analysis looks at the 'Strengths' and 'Weaknesses' inside the firm, and the 'Opportunities' and 'Threats' outside of it. The SWOT analysis is an important step for strategy formulation.
It helps to:

1. Identify one's strengths and weaknesses
2. Leverage opportunities aligned with one's interests
3. Plan for threats in future
4. Make efforts to reduce the impact of one's weaknesses

An interesting client case Samanta worked on involved a mobile-phone provider. The company had a market share of almost 18 per cent and was growing at a rapid pace. The low-cost-high-features strategy was working well. The company had hired Pinnacle to help it expand its growth potential. One of the weaknesses Samanta pointed out was the product innovation and design team slowing down and causing the new models to take more time getting to the market. Unfortunately, the client team didn't take the warning to address the issue seriously. As a result, three Chinese companies entered the market and came up with multiple brands at a cheaper price with comparable or better features. In just eighteen months, the client experienced a 50 per cent drop in market share.

Samanta also suggested leveraging one of the e-commerce platforms for a broader reach to potential buyers. The client dragged its feet in implementing the idea, since it already had a strong retail engine. However, new brands entering the market capitalized on the available technology and used multiple e-commerce platforms to conduct exclusive launches. Their reach broadened dramatically within a short period of time.

Often, a SWOT analysis done with strong data to back it up can help companies make wise decisions for the future.

PESTLE Analysis

The PESTLE analysis is a helpful tool in understanding five key elements of the external environment and how they impact an industry or a firm. These are Political, Economical, Technological, Legal and Environmental. The PESTLE analysis can work hand in hand with SWOT, since it helps identify the Opportunities and Threats an organization could face.

Samanta remembered a time when she used the PESTLE analysis to help an automobile manufacturer in South Korea. The Korean firm wanted a risk analysis of its operations over the next five years. This took place during the early stages of ride-sharing services such as Uber. Various analyses indicated that global trends could have a major influence on the firm's performance over the next five to ten years. Samanta's team recommended that the firm start preparing for change based on five trends that were directly predictive:

1. Increasingly, millennials were spending less on owning cars.
2. Ride-sharing services were growing, most likely in conjunction with millennials' preference.
3. The Internet of Things and other technology were set to have an impact on high-end cars in the near future.
4. The push for sustainable and environment-conscious technologies would mean stricter emission requirements, resulting in the need for electric/eco-friendly fuel-source usage.
5. The increase in the number of female drivers could result in a need for different design choices.

These trends opened up many opportunities for the firm. For example, the ride-sharing services would result in a larger market of drivers becoming car owners. The firm needed models in place that would fit its needs and budgets. Electric and hybrid technologies needed to be squeezed for more efficiency, which would open up a bigger market for the firm. It could think ahead of the curve on the impact of the Internet of Things (IoT) on cars and be pioneers in that area. However, if it took no action at all based on these trends, it could mean crippled growth in the medium-term.

Porter's Five Forces Analysis

Porter's Five Forces analysis[1] is one of the most well-known models of industry analysis. It helps assess the competition in the industry.

Samanta had worked hard to gain specialized knowledge in market-entry strategies. The Five Forces model was one of her go-to tools for assessing the feasibility of entering a new market. The five forces that shape an industry are:

1. Competition and rivalry in the industry
2. Threat of substitutes
3. Threat of new entrants
4. Bargaining power of suppliers
5. Bargaining power of customers

One of the most interesting clients Samanta worked with using this tool was a South East Asian airline attempting to enter the Indian market. The airline industry is considered one of the most unattractive industries in the world to enter. Competition is high—including price and service competition—substitutes exist, there are constantly new entrant possibilities, there are fewer suppliers in certain areas, which causes the suppliers to demand more control, and the customers themselves are very demanding. However, after doing a thorough analysis, Samanta recommended that the airline enter the low-cost market in the country. The main reasons included the growing number of air travellers, increased government investment in infrastructure and the flattening of fuel costs over time.

---

[1]   Michael E. Porter, 'The Five Competitive Forces That Shape Strategy', *Harvard Business Review*, January 2008, pp. 25–40.

An established player could make good use of these market dynamics as they applied their expertise to a new venture.

McKinsey's 7-S Model

McKinsey's 7-S[2] model helps organizations analyse the current status of an organization and identify the areas that require change. It also focuses on how to align the different elements of an organization to achieve greater effectiveness.

The seven elements of organizations are:

1. *Strategy:* This is the long-term differentiation of the organization in the competitive market. It defines how the organization is going to achieve its competitive advantage.
2. *Structure:* This defines how the organization is built. It includes how the organization is prepared to execute its strategy.
3. *Systems:* These are the processes and practices that help the organization run.
4. *Shared values:* These define how people work together and what the culture of the organization is.
5. *Style:* This is defined by how the leadership behaves and operates.
6. *Staff:* This denotes the type of staff and their general capabilities.
7. *Skills:* These include what the employees bring to the table.

---

[2]   Thomas J. Peters and Robert H. Waterman Jr, *In Search of Excellence: Lessons from America's Best-Run Companies,* Collins Business Essentials, 2012.

One of the advantages of this model is that it helps the consulting firm have a holistic approach towards project scoping.

One such project Samanta worked on involved a large Indian IT firm. The firm was losing its marketing leadership. High attrition rates at various levels were adding to the woes. Even the CEO and other top management had cycled through over the past two years. The illustration of the 7-S model for the client was as below:

Area	Details	Overall Alignment
Strategy	To be an innovative player in the market, providing cost-effective and modern solutions.	In line with market needs.
Structure	Hierarchical with multiple levels. Inward-looking structure. Has special structures for innovation.	Slows down innovation overall and often possesses overqualified managerial talent.
Systems	Highly process-oriented and often over-engineered in terms of processes.	Slow decision-making and often not nimble.
Shared values	Collaboration, customer focus, integrity, results-focused.	Stated values such as innovation and speed often not reflected in feedback.

Style	Traditional and often closed from others	Partial
Staff	Large number of employees often not motivated	Partial
Skills	Mix of old and modern technologies	Partial

The 7-S model helped paint a clear picture of where the organization could make changes to ensure the desired strategic alignment happened.

Based on the 7-S analysis, Pinnacle recommended the IT firm focus on the following:

- Re-evaluating the product and services portfolio to make it more market-aligned, from both a present-day and a future perspective.
- Employing benchmarking to create offerings with a more competitive advantage.
- Restructuring the organization to make it more market-focused, and reducing the hierarchy that hindered efficiency and innovation.
- Conducting a health survey to understand culture and leadership style. Focusing on change in leadership behaviours through coaching.
- Changing some of the key processes in sales and human resources to drive the right output.
- Employing a large-scale learning and development strategy to ensure employee capabilities and skills were in line with market demands.

Benchmarking

Benchmarking is an important element in most consulting assignments. The purpose of benchmarking is to provide an objective evaluation of a unit, business or company's current performance based on internal and external comparators, thus enabling a company to track progress and chart a path to success. Consultants bring value for their ability to provide external benchmarking to a company, sharing the benchmarks and best practices of comparators in the industry, including competitors, to help the company find ways to improve. With this data in hand, they can answer important questions such as 'Is my cost structure in line with the industry?', 'Is my pricing in line with the industry?' and 'Do I have comparable attrition rates to similar companies in the industry?'.

While some of the benchmarking questions are quantifiable, others are more practice-oriented, such as 'Does the industry follow a similar refund policy?', 'What marketing strategy do others in the industry follow?' and 'What are the employee-benefit policies of others in the industry?'.

Questions such as these help the organization be more competitive in the industry. Asking these kind of questions also helps the consultant challenge assumptions within the industry. For example, an organization might believe that a 10 per cent growth rate is low. However, an industry analysis might show that 10 per cent is better than most other players in the industry.

The data for benchmarking can come from four sources:

1. Published data by different agencies.
2. Publicly available best practices.
3. Data sourced for specific benchmarking.

4. Data that is available privately. Consulting firms will have access due to their association with the firms or various research studies conducted.

While benchmarking and sharing best practices is a standard part of consulting, clients themselves often become too focused on benchmarks. They can be misled by what the benchmarks appear to be saying and often fail to think outside the box in their effort to follow industry standards. On top of that, some of the benchmarks can be irrelevant to the company at that point in their journey. This is where the consultant can come in and guide the client in pursuing the right benchmarks and best practices.

Scenario-Planning

As Samanta progressed as a consultant, she realized that the main reason top management called in a consultant was because they think about the future and how to make it better. The situation she found repeated over and over again was that a higher-up in the company would be weighing multiple options and not be sure which decision to make. This was where she found scenario-planning helpful. Scenario-planning provided insight into the likelihood of failure or success on various strategic decision options.

Scenario-planning has multiple steps:

1. *Defining the issue/problem:* This is determining the key decision point. It usually starts with questions such as 'Should the company invest in a new product?', 'Should the company expand to another geographic region?' and 'Is this a good acquisition?'. There are many questions that can encapsulate the issue/problem and be the major focus of future decision-making.

2. *Understanding the factors involved:* This element identifies the various internal and external situations that can impact a decision in the future. For example, the company has decided to invest in a new market and there is a potential economic slowdown. What is the impact? At this stage, the factors that can impact the outcomes are charted out.

3. *Scenario-building:* This step involves crafting scenarios that are sensitive to the factors that influence the outcomes. Building the scenarios requires extensive experience and evaluating multiple possibilities—hence the consultant. The consultant then presents a wide range of scenarios, from the best case to the worst, to give the management team multiple options to work with.

4. *Indicators:* Indicators give clues to which scenarios might actually happen in real life. The indicators help management make amendments to its final decision and/ or reinforce it.

With the rise of various decision-making tools and greater access to statistics, scenario-planning and decision-making have become easier and more sophisticated. The analytics are more precise, making the task of predicting variables less overwhelming.

As a consultant, it's important to not be biased towards any one option beforehand. Favouring a specific option can lead to making positive assumptions about it, which could result in skewed data presented to the client. There is even more danger of this in qualitative scenario planning.

Scenario-planning also helps the company manage risk. Say the company decides to enter a market in a country new to its brand, but there's the risk of a change in government policy that could halt its operations. Scenario-planning identifies and highlights this risk. Similarly, if the decision to enter that market doesn't pay off, the resources of the company would be depleted. This, in turn, would lower the spending capabilities in its native country, leading to the company's poor performance on the whole. This is why scenario-planning is so helpful. It allows the company to construct a comprehensive risk-management strategy for moving forward.

An interesting project Samanta worked on involving scenario-planning took place during her interaction with a beer company in India. The company wanted an expansion plan and to enhance its supply-chain capabilities to match. The market trends showed that beer consumption in India was increasing and the market was growing beyond the big cities, into smaller towns. The company wanted to take advantage of this trend.

The first thing Samanta did was perform a thorough PESTLE analysis. She took a look at the political, economic, sociological, technical, legal and environmental factors that could impact the business. Below is the data Samanta uncovered:

Factors	Analysis
Political	The political environment showed that liquor, including beer, was often considered an 'anti-society' element. Politicians used liquor bans as a vote-garnering tool during elections. It was their way of proving they cared about the welfare of society, since the lower strata often bore the negative impact of liquor addiction.

Factors	Analysis
Economical	The increasing per capita income and discretionary spending of the middle class supported the consumption of beer in the country.
Sociological	The general society in India had a negative perception of liquor consumption, including beer. However, with the rise of beer consumption by the middleclass, social drinking was becoming a norm.
Technological	No high impact on beer production. However, better storage facilities were helping the industry, and more innovation around craft and draught beers made them more widely available.
Legal	Companies faced many legal cases with regulatory changes by the government in various states.
Environmental	Clean water is a major component of beer production and impacts quality. A major concern of the local society was the depletion of water resources near beer-production plants.

The PESTLE analysis helped identify the states in which the company should invest. Samanta recommended that the company stick to states with a strong middle class and which had at least one or two highly cosmopolitan cities. She then presented the various scenarios that could impact the market success, also pointing out the risks of prohibition.

While the company followed her recommendations on three of the locations, it overlooked the risk of prohibition on two additional locations because of the potential they offered. However, Samanta's predictions based on the scenario analysis were correct. After two and a half years, the new production facilities in the two states the company had chosen had to be shut down due to prohibition.

BCG Matrix, GE McKinsey Matrix and Ansoff Matrix

The BCG Matrix and GE McKinsey Matrix are some of the most popular tools for assessing the attractiveness of business portfolios, products and services in a company. Samanta studied these frameworks during her time at the management institute.

The BCG Matrix looked at a product or a business portfolio from a 2x2 matrix that assessed relative market share and growth. In terms of a business portfolio, companies need to invest in and nurture the high-growth and high-market-share categories. Companies need to sustain the cash cows and use their resources to further other business interests. High-growth-and-low-market-share portfolios, if nurtured well, could turn into future stars or cash cows. Low-growth-and-low-market-share portfolios need to be divested or restructured to enhance growth or market shares. A firm that has multiple businesses could effectively use the BCG matrix.

High Growth and Low Market Share (?)	High Growth and High Market Share (Stars)
Low Growth and Low Market Share (Dogs/Pets)	Low Growth and High Market Share (Cash Cows)

The GE McKinsey Matrix was a nine-box matrix that helped determine the priority of business units based on industry attractiveness and the strength of the particular business unit. While the industry attractiveness could be tracked by Porter's Five Forces or the PESTLE analyses, the strength of a specific business unit could have multiple factors that may not be as easy to track. Apart from the growth and market share, other factors could be the customer brand, strength of the products, customer loyalty and profitability.

Samanta was involved in an interesting project regarding a public-sector unit in Singapore. The company wanted to devise a strategy to double its revenues by enhancing its profitability over the next five years. The organization had diversified business interests that had evolved over the past thirty years based on opportunities in the market. The four main business areas included:

1. Industrial packaging
2. Logistics solutions
3. B2B e-commerce solutions
4. Luxury hotels and vacation services

The organization had started with the industrial-packaging and logistics-solutions businesses in the mid-1980s. The luxury hotels and vacation services were started ten years later, in the mid-1990s, when the Asian middle class had started using its disposable income for travelling and vacationing. The B2B e-commerce solutions business was the newest in the mix, at just two years old, and was built to emulate the Alibaba model in Singapore. The goal was to make the service available to the Asian markets.

Samanta's assignment was to look at the potential growth of each of the businesses within the conglomerate and come up with an effective five-year plan. She used her knowledge of the different frameworks to assess the attractiveness and growth potential of each of the businesses.

Using the BCG matrix, the businesses were categorized as below:

B2B E-commerce (?)	Nil (Stars)
Luxury Hotels and Vacation Services (Dogs/Pets)	Industrial Packaging and Logistics (Cash Cows)

B2B e-commerce was to be nurtured for the high growth and increase the market share. This could then be a star in their portfolio.

The analysis results of the company were similar with the McKinsey GE matrix. The industry-attractiveness analysis showed that the B2B e-commerce business had a moderately high level of industry attractiveness. Most of the other businesses had a low to medium level of attractiveness. It was clear that the industrial-packaging and logistics businesses were the strength of the organization. They had strong client relationships—especially with the government and public-sector organizations. They also had strong processes and technology to support their operations. The B2B e-commerce aspect of the company was still in its nascent stage and needed a lot more support to effectively compete and grow in the market. The luxury-hotels division was being weighed down by older properties and had to deal with the issue of ageing staff. Whether the business was worth perpetuating or not was in question.

The industrial-packaging and logistics businesses required some innovation to make them more efficient and profitable. The B2B e-commerce business needed more capabilities built within the firm. The luxury-hotels and vacation services were definitely the area where the company was losing its competitive advantage.

The second level of analysis was done using the Ansoff Matrix:

Present		Products	
		New	
Markets	Present	Market Penetration	Product Development
	New	Market Development	Diversification

Once the organization decided on the overall strategy on the future strategy of the various business units, the Ansoff Matrix looks at what could be done with each of the product lines, and future and current market plans. For example, the B2B e-commerce had opportunities to expand new market and also new product development.

One of the important elements of an effective strategy is making good choices. Making a choice and sticking with it isn't easy for even the best management teams. In Samanta's case, she performed a detailed analysis and provided the resulting recommendations on the best way forward to the top management. The gist of her recommendations were:

Industrial Packaging and Logistics	Enhance efficiencies and use technology-based improvements to ensure better service standards.
B2B E-Commerce	Build a partnership with a private player for agility and technology sponsorship.
Luxury Hotels and Vacation Services	Lease out the properties or have a licensing model.

Logically, the solutions made a lot of sense. However, it was important to determine whether a public-sector player could actionize them. Political and societal factors influenced the top management as well. On top of that, there was internal resistance to following the recommendations, since it could lead to job losses and the shrinking influence of some of the senior leadership team members.

Adrian Alex, the managing director of the firm, invited Samanta to a private meeting to discuss her recommendations. She noticed he hadn't been overly expressive when she had first given the presentation to the management team. She was looking forward to what he had to say in a more closed setting. They met for breakfast and a walk in Esplanade Park on a Friday morning. He was a man in his mid-fifties, an industry leader who commanded tremendous influence in the corporate circles in Singapore. It was also said that he was close to key government decision-makers.

There was a defining trait Samanta observed among senior leaders who effectively led their companies—humility coupled with a high level of competence. Adrian was one of those leaders, open and willing to listen. Samanta had met him to discuss the company twice before she had given the presentation. This time, he was eager to hear more about her recommendations, and also to share his view. Samanta knew that having such conversations with C-Suite executives was an important skill for a leading consultant to possess.

The discussion with Adrian was insightful. First, he asked her what she thought the core competence of each of the businesses was. The concept of core competence had gained a lot of popularity since it was first proposed by C.K. Prahalad and Gary Hamel. It focused on identifying the various skills and knowledge that gave a company advantage over its competitors. Samanta proposed that the industrial-packaging business's chief advantage was its ability to provide quality metal packaging at the best possible price. The business achieved this through its effective procurement practices and automated production. In the logistics-solutions division, the fleet of trucks and strong technology backbone allowed it to make optimized deliveries. The luxury-hotel and vacation services aspect relied on customized customer service to gain an advantage. Finally, the B2B e-commerce company was still finding its way but trying to build a more evolved technology platform that would have more features than the competition when it matured.

Adrian was in agreement with most of Samanta's views. Samanta knew that the idea zone of a successful conversation was where the consultant was able to educate the client and the client found the insights shared relevant.

'It's helpful for me to understand that the core competencies we have as a company aren't constant,' Adrian said. 'And they really are relative when considering the competition. Here in Singapore, we still work more or less like a private sector. We're answerable to our holding corporation. We have to ensure that we deliver the expected returns, but we still have to make most decisions on our own. It's a unique model that has kept enterprises in the Singaporean public sector successful.'

The frameworks and analysis Pinnacle provided through Samanta helped give direction to Adrian. Now it was just a question of how he and the management team would implement these changes within the different businesses. The company asked Pinnacle to continue guiding them through the process as they moved forward. This included creating a detailed plan for each of the businesses, as well as determining how to align the various partners involved in the process.

The main issue the top management faced was knowing if the recommendations were really feasible. There were already multiple obstacles to be faced in any public-sector enterprise, such as the current leadership team not wanting to deal with major changes, trying to obtain government buy-in and gathering the huge investment needed to make the changes.

This was where the capabilities Samanta had built over the years in financial acumen and change management came in handy.

The Fish Bone Diagram and Decision-Making Skills

The fish bone diagram, or the Ishikawa diagram, has its origins in the quality domain. It looks at the relationship between cause and effect.

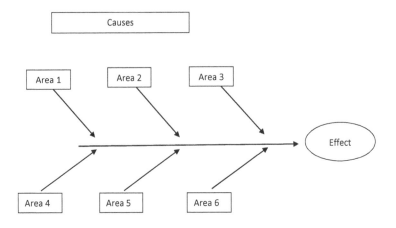

Samanta liked the fish bone diagram. She often thought of it as a simple way to discuss the problem at hand, since it enumerated the variables that could be causing the issue.

Samanta worked on a project for enhancing the profitability of an industry compressor organization. The organization had models that used two technologies. The traditional technology had high volume and market share but lower profitability. The new technology was more expensive but also had better features and better margins.

Now, the fish bone diagram for that looked like this:

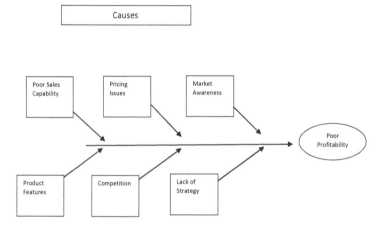

However, the sales team wasn't prioritizing upping the sales of the new technology models. They were afraid to go up against their competitors in the field, which, of course, led to fewer sales. This came up in the detailed analysis Samanta performed. The analysis provided action steps to take in each of the different areas as well. However, it was important to recognize the key issues impacting profitability. A simple tool Samanta used for situations such as this was called the '5 whys'.

In most cases, when using the 5 whys tool, the root cause of the problem is uncovered. However, this needs to be validated by data for the client to take it seriously.

Once the key challenge is identified, the client is given various recommendations on how to improve. The implementation and the change management associated with the same starts from here.

8

Financial Literacy

'One third of the candidates never make it to being a partner because of this, one third of partners never become successful because of this, and the other third become good because of this. Can you tell me what I am speaking about?'

This was a question from a partner who was part of the business-restructuring practice when he was speaking during the induction of Samanta and other consultants at Pinnacle. There were answers such as teamwork and conceptual knowledge given by the audience. One of the consultants, who had a finance background, spoke about business understanding and, more importantly, financial literacy. When the partner asked him to explain, he said, 'A lot about a business can be understood by going through a company's financial statements. A good consultant should be able to appreciate the finance part of the company. It shows the performance and the challenges, and most management efforts are decided based on this.'

The partner was quite impressed and told him that the financial reports of a company were definitely like one's health check-up reports. They were akin to seeing the outcomes of all that had been happening in the company and its business.

The second question the partner asked was simple: 'Do you have the habit of reading the annual reports of companies?' Many of them had done this during their finance courses at their institutes—more as a matter of curriculum than any genuine interest. Samanta, however, was not in the same assemblage. 'I do read annual reports on a regular basis. They used to give me a lot of fodder on the companies when I used to invest in stock markets,' she said.

Most of the companies that Samanta had worked with were either publicly listed or large firms that were privately held. Financial analysis could show why somebody was taking certain management decisions. Change of strategy, too, was often the result of a company's financial performance or expected financial performance.

When Samanta was an engagement manager at Pinnacle, she was entrusted with making a proposal for creating a growth strategy that enabled an Indian automobile-battery company to grow above the industry average. The chairman's message in the annual report showed they were planning to grow at 15 per cent that particular year with a differentiated strategy. This was interesting because when Samanta analysed their last three years' financial performance, the company had grown at an average of 8.5 per cent in terms of revenues and 3–4 per cent in terms of net profits. The data showed the company needed to grow at 1.76 times of the previous year to adhere to the promise made to the shareholders. A look at the company's assets also showed capital investments made in the previous two years. The chairman's comments mentioned that the company was investing in a large factory that would enhance the overall capacity of product manufacturing.

In the 'Management Development and Analysis' section of the financial statements, the company spoke about the macroeconomic and industry trends that were going to impact the business both positively and negatively. There were some striking trends that could be seen in the report. The economic growth was slowing down and there was a potential slowdown in the automobile industry due to changes in emission norms and overall market sentiments. The company was opening up new sectors to explore as markets. Overall, there were pressures on pricing and the competitive environment was seen as more difficult for the company. While the chairman's message was positive of a recovery and spoke about future growth, the general sentiments in terms of economy and industry were not very positive.

Samanta looked at various aspects of the business that had worked well for the company. The annual report mentioned the various business opportunities that the company had leveraged till then. They were strong in the 'original equipment' domain, with an almost 30 per cent market share in the country, and in the after-market segment, the company spoke of having around a 20 per cent market share, and almost 10 per cent of its business came from exports.

The profit and loss statement showed the revenues and the expenses associated with the company. Interestingly, the cost of materials was around 65 per cent for the company while the employee costs were less than 5 per cent. The data, when compared to industry peers, showed that the company was in line on the cost of materials and was 3–4 percentage points below the industry average on the employee costs.

The profit and loss statement also 'showed a change in inventories of finished goods'. The analysis of the data showed that percentage of unsold stocks had increased over the previous year. This also possibly indicated that the company had produced more than planned or that sales had not happened as expected.

Further analysis of the balance sheet of the annual report showed that the capital work in progress (it could be factories or any new project that would involve capital investment) was almost five times the profits earned for the year. This indicated that the company was better on production capacity augmentation by adding new factories.

The next step was to look at some of the financial ratios that gave a perspective on how well the company had done. The typical ratios that are used to analyse the company were:

Leverage Ratios: These ratios look at how a company is leveraged. That means how much debt is used to finance the company's operations. Leverage ratios can speak about how sustainable the company is.

Operating Ratios: This looks at how effectively a company is leveraging its assets into revenues. The two ratios that caught Samanta's attention were the 'inventory turnover' and the 'inventory number of days'. The inventory turnover is the cost of goods sold/average inventory, and the inventory number of days is 365/inventory turnover. Samanta saw the inventory turnover was lower and that maybe she needed to compare it with other industry peers. This ratio is definitely a reflection of lack of alignment or agility in managing finished goods inventory vis-à-vis sales demand. Sales and production planning may have to be better aligned in a company that has inefficiencies in this ratio.

Profitability Ratios: This looks at how effective a company is in managing profits. For example, one of the profitability ratios is the PAT (profit after tax) margin. This ratio looks at PAT/revenue. The ratio can help one understand what percentage of the revenue the company finally gets to keep after operating expenses and taxes.

Valuation Ratios: This looks at how attractive it is to hold stock of the company. The one that caught Samanta's attention here was the P/E ratio. That is the current share price/earnings per share. The company had a high P/E ratio—hovering around 38. A P/E ratio of more than 30 generally shows an overvalued share. It means that the market has already (maybe even temporarily) believed in the better prospects of the company and, clearly, the promoters or the management team would be looking at enhancing its revenues and, of course, profitability.

Another ratio that can be considered one of the most crucial in understanding a company's business is its return on equity (RoE). The ratios look at the return to the shareholders, who are ultimately the owners of the company. Financial gurus consider it an important ratio to look at. The DuPont framework (shown below), defined by the DuPont Corporation, is considered a good guide to looking at different components of RoE.

The DuPont framework is defined as:

$$\boxed{\text{Dupont}} = \boxed{\text{Profitability}} \times \boxed{\text{Productivity}} \times \boxed{\text{Leverage}}$$

Profitability is measured as the net profit/revenue, productivity as revenue/assets, and leverage as assets/shareholder equity. The RoE, as per the DuPont framework, can be used to analyse the comparative position of the company vis-à-vis the industry. The framework also let us understand where the RoE is coming from—profitability, productivity or leverage. Each of these components also lets us analyse where a company is underperforming. A company, in general, is in a good position if the RoE is coming from profitability and productivity.

Samanta gained a good understanding of the business and its industry by studying the company's financial statements. The fundamental analysis helps to see through the business in great detail. For a consultant, it definitely helps to get closer to the mindset of the promoter.

Industry and Financial Statements

It was during one of the sessions that Samanta attended at Pinnacle that a partner took up a Harvard case to explain how financial statements could describe industry characteristics. The case was written by Mihir Desai, William Fruhan and Elizabeth Meyer,[1] all professors at Harvard Business School. The case shared balance sheet percentages of assets, liabilities and shareholders' equity, and financial ratios of about fourteen companies without naming them. It then shared the company names and the industry for the participants to match.

It is interesting to see how assets are distributed depending on the industry or the kind of liabilities a company might have. A lot of the industry characteristics are reflected in the balance sheets as well. It is also often easy to understand what kind of operations a company has looking at its balance sheet. For example, a company that is into service might have an almost zero inventory, compared to one that is involved in production.

---

[1] Mihir A. Desai, William E. Fruhan Jr and Elizabeth A. Meyer, 'The Case of the Unidentified Industries—2013', *Harvard Business School Publications*, 2013.

Similarly, banks have one of the largest receivable collection periods. The receivables are the repayment to the loans given to customers. The quality of the assets here are an important aspect for a bank's health. Each industry has its own characteristics and a company's balance sheets give the one studying them a lot of interesting insights. It gave Samanta some very interesting perspectives of industry financial benchmarks, cost parameters and profitability aspects.

Samanta always believed that a good consultant is able to integrate the financial concepts with their functional knowledge. She was once discussing a supply chain project with a team member. She went ahead to explain with an example. 'Inventory management has a direct impact on cash flow. Any decision has an impact on multiple aspects, and finance is one part of that system. A company may choose to reduce the inventory levels, reduce the credit period to its buyers or increase the payable period to its vendors. All three help increase the cash flow/position in the company. However, there are business forces that can act against them. A company might face the risk of inventory run-out, buyers going to rivals or vendors not being interested in selling to it. An ideal situation is often the balance of the business context, functional priorities and the financial outcome.

'Financial analysis is a key skill in making most business decisions. A good consultant is able to connect recommendations to financial outcomes to share business RoI in clear terms. Similarly, keeping financial aspects in mind can help one make strategic choices, such as organic growth, mergers and acquisitions, geographical expansion and decisions to lay off certain businesses. Long-term versus short-term financial impacts is a criterion to choose a strategy. A connect to financial outcomes/impact is also an important decision-making criterion by business stakeholders, and a consulting leader should be able to appreciate this.'

9

The Gloom and Back

'Sammy!'

Samanta jerked her head up to look at Jacob. What had he been saying?

Jacob raised an eyebrow. 'I know losing the promotion has left you reeling, but this isn't the time to fall apart. You can learn from this and come back stronger.'

She nodded, fidgeting with her bracelet, but the thought that had been plaguing her since the lost promotion nagged at her again. Would her self-confidence ever return? Or was she destined to wander through her career like a lost star floating through space?

'Listen,' Jacob said, 'everyone goes through this phase at least once in their career. I remember when I was struggling to manage my team and getting fed up with all the travel. It got so bad that I wound up leaving Pinnacle because of it.' He clasped his hands together and looked at the floor. 'I'll be honest—it was difficult to leave. The brand, the money, working with some of the best minds in the industry and, of course, friends such as you made it a tough decision.

But I think I found my mojo here with the private equity firm, so I don't regret my choice. I'm good with numbers and can analyse businesses pretty well. I find that working with the top management teams of different organizations has really helped me.' He cocked his head. 'Have you considered making a switch?'

A smile tugged at the corners of Samanta's mouth. 'Are you offering me a job?' she said, winking.

Jacob chuckled. 'You're always welcome to join us. Who would say no to a star like you?'

Samanta allowed herself a laugh and sat back in her chair. She could tell Jacob was trying to tread carefully, even though they'd been friends for years. She was sure he knew how much she hated too much advice, and appreciated him not laying it on too thick.

Jacob spread his hands. 'I guess it's just hard for me to see you like this. You're the hardest worker I've seen pass through Pinnacle's doors, and I don't want you to do anything you'll regret down the road.'

Samanta nodded and took a sip from her latte. It wasn't giving her the boost she hoped it would. And heaven knew she needed one. 'Do you think I should continue at Pinnacle?'

Jacob's eyebrows rose. 'Good question. Let me ask you what you were asked when you first joined. Why consulting? And why Pinnacle? What has really kept you there?'

'Are you interviewing me again, Jake?'

He only grinned.

'Well,' she said, 'I love applying knowledge, helping my clients succeed and, of course, mentoring my team.' She shrugged. 'I'm also seen as an expert in two or three areas, and I feel proud of that.'

Jacob leaned forward in his chair. 'And how are you feeling now?'

She sighed. 'I feel like a nobody in the firm. I've never felt so average in my life. It feels like all the effort I've put into my career up to this point has been wasted. And how will my colleagues look at me now? As a mediocre consultant?'

Jacob shifted in his chair and scratched the back of his neck. Samanta could tell she was making him uncomfortable. She had never talked like this to him before. He must be wondering how a once-confident consultant was now talking like a loser.

'Sammy, the path you're on right now could quite possibly end with you leaving Pinnacle. I'm not sure if that's the right direction to take, but let's explore it together.' He pulled a piece of paper out from his pocket and started drawing on it. Samanta waited for him to finish. He was a master at explaining concepts, and she was looking forward to what he had to share.

He showed Samanta what he was adding to the paper. 'Imagine you're standing between two mirrors. Your peers and seniors see you in one of them, and you see yourself in the other. Using a point or two from what Ivan had shared with you on your strengths and development areas, here's what we have.'

Samanta's Self-View	Others' View
Hard-working	Needs to innovate
Good people-management skills	Needs to go beyond clients and team
Excellent communicator	Needs to build a personal brand
Expert in many areas	Needs to cultivate a learner's mindset and grow in new areas

'You're a fighter, Sammy. And I think you have an opportunity here to push yourself to the next level. What do you think?'

Samanta frowned and set her latte down on the coffee table—hard. 'I already feel inadequate, and you drop this on me? You're supposed to motivate me!'

The chair squeaked as Jacob leaned forward. 'Think about your fencing practice. You didn't play the same at the state level as you did in the nationals. And you certainly didn't play at the same level when you represented your country. Why else do you think the world's best sportspeople have coaches? They're essential to sharpening one's skills. You have some great skills yourself, Sammy. You just need to develop some new ones too.'

This time Samanta nodded. Just the mention of fencing made her heart race and brought her sporting spirit flooding back.

Jacob sat back in his chair. 'I had an informal chat with one of the senior partners a little while back, and we spoke about you. I told him how we've known each other for years and how we are from the same institute. The partner was all praise about you, talking about how well you manage your clients and mentor your team, and, of course, raving about your strong work ethic. But I find it insightful that he ended by saying, "I just wish she would show more leadership and originality. She needs to create her own space." What do you think about that?'

She nodded. 'It's what Ivan told me. Be original, take risks, be yourself and build a personal brand. But I thought I already was original.'

'In our career, self-doubt and a feeling of inadequacy crop up now and again. I look at them as wake-up calls. As soon as I realized I wasn't good at managing my team and that I hated the routine, I called it quits. I simply didn't want to put in the effort to become a people's champion. Now, the question before you is whether you are willing to better yourself.'

Samanta frowned. She wasn't sure. It had been hard enough to reach her current station. Doing more didn't sound very appealing.

Jacob seemed to sense her uncertainty. 'Tell you what. Let's take some time and create a career-development plan specifically for you. Put a defined time frame on it and, hopefully, it will help you see your way into the future. You write it, and I'll help you craft it.'

Samanta took the last sip of her latte. This was going to be intense. She felt more like brooding over the past than facing the future, but, maybe, as Jacob said, it would help her see her way into the future.

Keeping in mind her career objective of becoming a partner in less than two years and, if that didn't work out, look for alternative career options, this is what they came up with:

Goal	Steps
Build personal brand	• Actively participate in industry forums and take on voluntary roles. • Share thought leadership with industry leaders.
Innovate	• Take risks and build a new business portfolio for Pinnacle. • Cultivate new capabilities for self and firm.
Explore new markets	• Create opportunities with existing as well as new clients for new capabilities.

Samanta looked at what she had written and lowered her brows. 'I'm going to earn my stripes. I'll do my best at Pinnacle for a couple of more years, and if it doesn't work out, I'll find a new path.'

* * *

Samanta sat back in her office chair and nodded to herself. Her confidence had begun to return since her meeting with Jacob. Their talk and the plan she had walked away with were giving her new purpose. The lost promotion was in the past, where it belonged, and now she could focus on building the support she would need to accomplish her plan.

Over the next several weeks, she studied the new solutions and practices Pinnacle was proposing to its clients around the globe. These new areas meant a lot of future prospects for the firm. Being an expert in market-entry strategies came in handy for Samanta. It made her wonder if Ivan and Aekta had spoken prophetically. She realized she would have had no clue how to bring a new practice to a new territory if not for their instructions. A saying from Steve Jobs came to mind: 'The various happenings in your life and career are in one way or another linked to the future.'

Since her meeting with Jacob, she had decided to reinvent herself. She would get out of this mid-career crisis and find purpose and excitement. Her initial thought was to relocate to a new country, create a business proposition and build an entire practice from scratch. It was a bold move but she felt confident she could make it work. Before making any major decisions, though, she consulted her husband. After explaining her plan to Abe and mentioning she was thinking of relocating to Singapore, he had been game. As a tech entrepreneur, a move wouldn't affect his career much, except perhaps adding a bit more travel.

In this early planning stage, Samanta took a leaf from the advice Hamid had given her during her early days at Pinnacle: 'Build your coalition for success.' She had forgotten that golden advice in the whirlwind of life, but she was grateful it came back to her now.

Three questions also came to mind:

1. How will I sell this new plan?
2. Who are the stakeholders that matter?
3. What are the metrics of success? Why should the firm agree to her proposition?

Samanta had worked on bringing the firm's analytics practice to India. It had helped the firm build its own capabilities and showcase its approach to making sense of large data in management decision-making. The experience had taught her a lot. She believed that data analytics would play a big role in the industry in future. Many organizations didn't know how to build these capabilities into their structure. In that way, it was a sweet spot. The organizations saw the value of implementing data analytics but needed help either figuring out how or someone to process the analytics for them. Pinnacle did both. They consulted on how an organization could build these processes into their business, and through their service centre in India, were able to process some of the analytics themselves as a third party.

Samanta reflected on how Pinnacle had masterfully found and embraced its sweet spot. There were sweet spots in all organizations, consulting or otherwise, but the key with any of them was to find an area where interest and capabilities intersected. Instead of being lulled into ignorance through success and staying in its comfort zone, Pinnacle had seized the opportunity before it, and now enjoyed exciting returns on its investment. Samanta wondered if perhaps her denied promotion was allowing her to enjoy that same kind of excitement as she focused on her future prospects.

She took the next step in her plan by meeting with the country leader and managing partner in Singapore. He not only led the branch in Singapore but oversaw the entire South East Asia region.

Georgie, as his colleagues called him, was not an easy customer. He had learnt about Samanta's disappointment over being denied the promotion and his first response after she explained her plan was, 'Is this an escape route?'

Samanta knew this would be the first question many people would ask, but years of consulting had taught her how to react in this kind of situation.

'Georgie,' she said, 'I have a business proposition based on the work I've done in India. The US team wants to expand the analytics business and I'm wondering about the possibilities in South East Asia in collaboration with India.'

She showed him several specific points on the business potential for the coming year, all backed up with hard data. 'I can send you a detailed presentation if you like,' she said. 'My only condition for this venture is that I lead it while working directly with you. What do you say?'

Georgie's face crinkled in thought for a moment. Then he laughed. 'Not even clients say no to you. How can I?'

She smiled. Maybe things would change, after all.

Georgie leaned forward in his chair. 'How will you adjust to the new environment and country?'

Samanta nodded. 'I've already discussed this idea with some of the key stakeholders and partners in Singapore, and have gained some valuable feedback. I also understand how our potential clients think, since I've collaborated with many of them in the past. Living in a new country is going to be a challenge, but working with a more diverse environment won't be. I'm open to learning and will make this work.'

* * *

The next year that unfolded was a consultant's dream. Samanta went from being an expert in her field to developing as a business leader. She took the first three months to transition out of her former job before joining the Singapore office. When she entered her new workplace, she set to work building the inter-office network and delegating responsibilities so that every client was served with excellence.

At the start of the year, when it became clear that she was going to pursue building a new business, Samanta met Ivan for a mentoring session.

'The biggest success in my life,' Ivan said, 'was that I made our European revenues quadruple in six years. Nobody would've thought I could do it. But, looking back, I had three things going for me—belief, a plan and hard work.' He smiled. 'And, of course, a little bit of luck.'

Samanta smiled too.

Ivan continued. 'You've set clear goals for this venture. Believe in those goals. Create a solid plan to achieve them. And, most importantly, focus and work hard at accomplishing them. I know you can create goals, and you should have no problem believing in them and helping others do the same, but you'll need to be most intentional about crafting an effective plan. How are you going to make your goals happen? Your plan should tackle the "blue oceans" in the market. Other players are already starting to provide similar services to what you're offering and will soon be established in Singapore. How are you going to compete? And don't just focus on the next year—think two or three years out too.'

After their meeting, Samanta created her five-point agenda before making the final decision to commit to the venture:

Define the market	Identify potential buyers in the market and create business cases.
Decide which areas to focus on	While analytics is a massive space, identify the potential functional/industry areas, such as finance, energy and public health.
Spread the word	Reach out to the market by spreading thought leadership.
Build pilot	Develop pilots in the market. Do projects that can be case studies to show other potential clients.
Build deep engagements	Develop at least five deep engagements that are individually more than $1 million in revenue.

Samanta drew it like a Venn diagram:

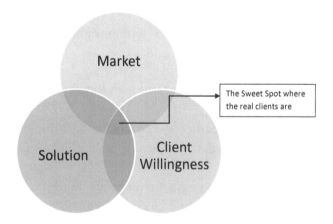

The market Samanta was interested in was similar to the market targeted by Pinnacle as part of its regular consulting offerings. Some of the businesses in the market would be interested in Pinnacle's solutions but only a few would be willing to actually put in the time and money necessary to implement them.

Samanta's job was showcasing the solutions in a way that created the needed willingness from the client. Samanta crafted a five-step agenda to help her accomplish her goal:

Industries	Identify the industries most likely to need the services.
Companies	Identify companies that would be interested based on certain parameters.
Decision-makers	Identify and influence the decision-makers.
Provide a value proposition	What would be the return on investment (RoI) for the adopting organization?
Build deeper relationships	Provide further solutions that are relevant to the client.

Samanta's analysis provided her with insights for moving forward:

1. Focus on the financial sector, the government, oil and gas, and pharmaceuticals.
2. List of top ten companies by turnover and profitability.
3. List of top decision-makers, including the CEO/CFO/CIO of organizations.
4. Solutions to enhance competitiveness on multiple fronts, including costs, pricing and customer segmentation.

She also realized that 60 per cent of these companies had some form of relationship with Pinnacle, whether it was in the present or at some point in the past.

Finally, she made it to Singapore with a dream of setting up a multimillion-dollar practice. But how did one crack a market like that? Pinnacle wasn't exactly known for analytics consulting. The partners who already had relationships with the clients wouldn't be thrilled with the idea of proposing new solutions. They had already charted out clear plans for their clients to follow and would view the new solutions as distractions. It certainly wouldn't be easy to change their minds. But she needed them on board if she were to have any hope of succeeding.

Samanta found that whenever she was stuck, she often came up with the best solutions. She decided to address the problem in a big way. She talked Georgie and the analytics practice leader in the US into giving her a substantial marketing budget. The first programme she organized was a mega thought-leadership event, where the CXOs from her target clients were invited. Each of the key partners played a role in the event. Samanta provided them with talking points to help them engage with their clients. She also did a preliminary survey with the CXOs to identify the challenges they faced that could be solved by the analytics solutions and geared the rest of the event towards dealing with those challenges. The presence of more than seventy CXOs definitely made an impact on the minds of potential clients.

The next six months were busy with client meetings and helping the partners tell the compelling story she had crafted. At the end of eight months, Samanta had four client engagements in the bag, which was a big win. The main thing she took away from the experience was to never plan small. If someone advised testing the market to see what happened, they were thinking too small. Aiming for the market potential was the key to business growth.

Something else Samanta learnt during this period was the art of storytelling. More than just the standard business storytelling, this was the art of telling transformational stories through data analytics. She used the four big projects she had bagged as success stories she could share with other potential clients. Over the years, Samanta had mastered the art of problem-solving and providing guidance in the creation of clear solutions. However, when it came to explaining to a CXO why they needed to build an analytics infrastructure into their company, it was necessary to present a strong business outcome backed by case studies. Coming from a non-analytics but strong business background, Samanta also knew it would be important to build credibility in this area.

Samanta went to the New York office for two months and paid close attention to how she functioned in a large analytics project the team was engaged in. She learnt the strategic aspect of the project in detail and how to properly execute those strategies. She also became certified in the subject through an MIT remote-learning course. Samanta spoke with more confidence on the subject after this eye-opening stint.

Storytelling was more appealing when Samanta incorporated real case studies, depth of knowledge about the subject and her newly found confidence into her interactions with potential clients. There were three elements she found important to include in her stories: a great narrative (a case study, an incident or a discussion), relevant characters and a clear business outcome. She started the stories with something such as, 'Here's an example of a leading financial services company and how it improved the acquisition of high-net-worth individuals using data analytics.' Or, 'Here's how a major city in the US reduced traffic accidents through data analysis.'

Clients were attracted to the realistic stories Samanta shared. To make the stories even more relatable, Samanta named and described the stakeholders involved to give them character. She portrayed how they positively influenced business or managed a challenge. And she did her best to make the narratives mirror the clients' situations to create contextual relevance. As she told the stories, she made use of her voice and gestures to emphasize key points and keep the clients engaged. These encounters often ended with a client sharing their problems in detail and asking Samanta to propose a solution for them on the spot.

Samanta also wrote an article with the US and European practice leaders on the future of data analytics and industry 4.0. The article shared how a data-driven approach would be key to the future of the industry. As the article was circulated, it established Samanta as a thought leader among potential clients.

At the end of a year and a half in Singapore, Samanta had achieved the following:

1. Deep practice leadership
2. Client networks
3. Market and business growth through innovation
4. Deep influence with the firm
5. Ability to take calculated risks

Looking back, she was satisfied with her achievements, especially her growth in the area of risk-taking, which she considered to be the most important. And she had almost reached the point where she had achieved everything Ivan had suggested. Life was looking up.

* * *

Understanding a Practice: Analytics Consulting, as told by Sudeep K. Krishnan, analytics leader, EXL Analytics

In today's world, the quantity and variety of data available for organizational decision-making is unparalleled and critical to creating value. This value creation happens through the combination of the right minds and the relevant tools. Data analytics is the organizational practice leveraging data and developing analytics-driven strategy implementation. Organization-wide analytics initiatives help minimize risks, optimize costs, identify new areas of growth and profitability, and understand customer needs.

So what does an analytics consultant normally do and what are the essential skills required to succeed in the role? The presence of an analytics consultant at an organ-transplant surgery or a blow-out-preventer (BOP) maintenance session in an oil well shows the unprecedented growth of this line of consulting. It was definitely not business as usual a few years back. While the analytics practice in itself and the importance of it within organizations are maturing, analytics consultants work closely with business partners to identify and capture benefits from data. While data analytics is the practice of using tools, techniques and statistical methods to identify meaningful patterns from large data, the main role an analytics consultant plays is to make everyone better decision-makers—from executives to specialists, and from front-line customer-facing agents to the customers themselves.

It is not just the quality or the quantity of data that can help businesses, it is the people who can interpret data and derive meaningful insights for in-depth understanding of the business. However, before understanding the role business acumen plays, it is essential to be aware that there are no industry-level standards or definitions on analytics. Even the terminologies for this group vary from organization to organization. The common names include business intelligence, big data, reporting and analytics, and data science, and these groups normally cover data management, analysis, modelling and development of dashboards.

To be successful in this practice, it is essential to have the right skillsets and to be able to match them with the scope of analytics in the client environment, helping organizations understand the need for analytics consulting. Usually, there are no out-of-the-box solutions that work in a variety of environments, and human skills that are contextually relevant are very important. Consulting approach really helps make customized analytics solutions for clients.

Figure: Progression on Data Analytics

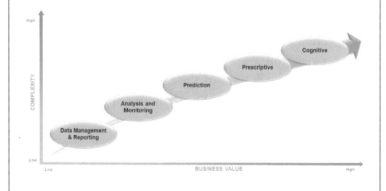

The introduction of data management and reporting lays the foundation of data analytics in any organization. This makes data available for basic queries, reporting and search functions. Organizations can typically answer 'what happened' and react to business situations with focused reporting. Organizations mature to answer questions such as 'why it happened' or 'what is happening' in real time with scorecards, dashboards and basic data models for analysis. However, the real complexity of data analytics and value start with predictive models and forecasting. Organizations become ready to predict what might happen in future. Thus, data and patterns enable organizations to control the future. Optimization models, digital transformation and business-process changes resulting from analytics help in prescriptive maturity and help the organizations learn what they need to do in future. The highest level of maturity happens with true cognitive skills when human and technology skills are augmented through artificial intelligence. Artificial intelligence is again a broad area, covering big data, machine-learning, natural language process, robotic process automation and analytics-driven transformation. With these emerging technologies, an analytics consultant not only works with clients and a large volume of data but also with digital workers, bots and other artificially intelligent systems, and quantifies a huge volume of data with the help of these systems.

The level of maturity and need of data analytics varies across sectors. Some of the key domains utilizing data analytics include:

- *Banking and Finance:* Artificial intelligence, blockchain and other areas of advanced analytics are being fully utilized in the financial sector. These institutions become more customer-focused and competitive, and make better investment decisions with the help of analytics. Curbing fraud, reducing risk and improving baseline profit are focus areas with analytics in this domain.
- *Healthcare:* Better patient outcomes, reduction in cost and patient risk, and equipping all parties in healthcare providing holistic and personalized treatments to patients are some of the reasons that can be attributed to data-based analytics interventions in healthcare.
- *Retail:* This is a sector heavily focused on consumer data and behaviour. Data analytics help retailers understand buying behaviour and prediction of demand, and influence consumer purchasing behaviour. The improvement of inventory, customer experience and personalized treatment, along with the optimization of overall cost, are outcomes of leveraging data in this sector.
- *Insurance:* In-depth customer-focused data analytics help insurance firms with the underwriting process and improved claims processing.
- *Travel:* Supply chain services, procurement and logistics through optimization, seasonal trend analysis and customer-expectations management are key factors explored in this sector, and advanced analytics is used to push preferences to customers.
- *Utilities:* From electric grids to asset data and from customer experience to cost optimization and marketing activities, the application of analytics in

the utility industry is not new and has been evolving over the past few years. Most of the optimization results achieved with the help of data enable organizations in the industry stay competitive and relevant to customers.

For an analytics consultant to succeed, it is essential for them to understand the business context in the domain of service. These contexts make the role of a consultant relevant in an oil well where a novel technique of data extrapolation is required to predict downtime or in an organ-transplant process to predict the survival of graft, which, in turn, affects the facility scoring by a government regulatory body. Their primary and key focus is to deliver substantial value through data. For the consultants, it might be relevant to be domain specialists rather than having platform or tool specialization. While it may be great to have knowledge of multi-variate or survival analysis, it is essential to know how to apply this in a client context. Hence, it is essential to understand business processes, pitfalls and pain points for clients, and understand that these data-based insights are only one of the key inputs. It becomes essential for a consultant to go in with a neutral view on the business problem than being judgemental. While in many cases, instincts of domain experts may hold, the stakeholders' expectation management and non-manipulation of data are key to success in this role. Soft skills and data-based storytelling capabilities become germane to an analytics consultant and how the value of data specific to a context is educated to a client can have potential impact on the strategic decisions being made.

Even though leaders and practitioners may be aware of growth of the area as analytics, they may not be aware of the role data analytics can play in their industries or domain of expertise. A physician or a geologist may not be able to comprehend the fact that a machine or an algorithm can do their jobs. It is essential to understand that data capabilities can only complement capabilities of such specialists, and an important role an analytics consultant plays is generating awareness and making client organizations understand the need for leveraging data for driving strategy. This typically happens when insights are tied with value. When the outcomes of the analysis are clear, clients normally understand the impact of recommendations driven by data. The ability to apply domain/business knowledge and articulation of the RoI can really help a consultant make an impact. This will also help decision-makers compare cost of implementation and help get support from executive leadership.

Analytics practice should hence be adopted across the organization as a horizontal practice complementing other verticals. When organizations start to invest heavily in data and analytics practice development, there are typically multiple partners involved—including data-management partners and business consulting firms.

It is also important to adapt to the rapidly changing environment and improvements in the area. There are faster data-processing tools, data-management solutions such as cloud technologies, and automated tools for insight generation. Another key success factor for an analytics consultant is to be tool-agnostic but with the ability to be flexible to use tools and techniques relevant to a client. With higher focus on the practice and increasing funding to support analytics as a practice, the line of analytics consulting will continue to grow. The abilities of a consultant to communicate complex insights derived from data and being the link between high-end technologies and clients may drive their success.

10

Standing on the Crest

'How does it feel?' Ivan said, looking at Samanta.

She shrugged. 'Normal. I don't feel anything has changed.'

Ivan stared at her, head cocked. He looked surprised at her lack of excitement.

'Being promoted to partner is important to me, don't get me wrong,' Samanta hurried to clarify, 'but the past year and a half has provided the learning that made it possible for me to excel so quickly. I'm more grateful for that.'

He nodded. 'The journey is where growth happens.'

'Exactly,' she said. 'The decision to select me as a partner was unanimous. I had all the right credentials. They were impressed with what I have accomplished since being turned down for the promotion last time. The new me is more mature, more confident. I charted and followed my own path and have grown my list of achievements within the firm.' She leaned forward in her chair. 'I think this is going to be the start of a new journey in my career. It sounds exciting to be a partner, and it certainly earns me more respect among my co-workers and clients, but there's also more responsibility. What do you think? How do I need to change?'

Ivan nodded thoughtfully before responding. 'You've seen many partners at the firm. Some great, some good and others just average. What do you admire about the great partners? And just remember, at the end of the day, you'll have to pursue your own path.'

She thought for a moment. 'I've watched many of the partners closely. Most were excellent communicators, built deep relationships, had a knack for getting business, built great teams and were considered experts in their field. While most of them shared the values our firm stands for—supporting each other, protecting our brand, delivering excellence—each one had a shade of their own in terms of strength. For example, KK is a great relationship builder. His primary way of getting more business is through relationships and the way he leverages the Pinnacle brand. And there's no doubt that he's good in his field. But I don't think he stresses about that.

'Then there's Hamid. He is constantly working to develop his expertise. He wants to be seen as an adviser. He always wants to come across as an expert with the client.

'There are also other partners who are loved by their teams. They are great mentors and teachers. Consultants love to work with them. They help guide these consultants in their career journeys. As far as these three areas are concerned, I think I'm good at what I do—I've built good relationships over time and I'm not so bad at leading others. As you mentioned before, I need to make up my mind and decide what my brand should be inside and outside the firm.'

Samanta had seen the other side of the partners as well. Some of them came across as arrogant with the clients, and even with team members. They had a high opinion of themselves and often sounded narcissistic. They tended to overlook their own flaws, didn't appreciate honest feedback and often required praise and acknowledgment to feed their egos. More often than not, the 'know-it-all' attitude and poor judgement of self and others led to inevitable mistakes—and their downfall. She remembered working with a senior partner in the firm who had a great network and was a star in his domain. He was very confident and had no qualms about praising himself. However, he was oblivious to how others perceived him and always sought validation. Samanta saw many like him in the consulting world. The sense of importance they received from clients, their elevated role in the firm and their vast networks tended to make them arrogant. However, their behaviour often earned them negative reputations that eventually caused conflict in their workplaces or with their clients.

'The business you bring, your network, your insights and leadership are all important,' Ivan said. 'But I would say that, in consulting, the most important aspect is your reputation. That's the foundation of everything. You do not choose your success, but you can choose your reputation. I crafted an interesting pyramid outlining the construction of a positive reputation.'

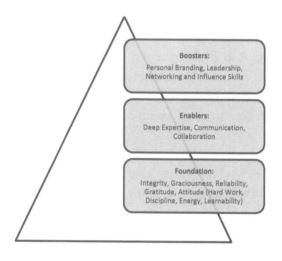

'At this point in your journey, I'm sure most of the foundation and enablers are in place. You'll still need to keep maintaining those areas, of course. To boost your reputation, you'll need to focus on developing elements such as your personal branding, coaching and supporting others, and building your reputation in the industry circle as a consultant with deep expertise.'

Samanta folded her arms and listened. This was insightful. Ivan had a lot of experience in this area.

He continued, 'Personal branding focuses on your reputation beyond the firm you represent. Over time, your unique skills and ability to deliver value can help build your brand.' The following grid can really help us spot the personal brand of professionals:

Hollow: Poor Value Addition and High Branding	Stars: Great Value Addition and Branding
Unknown	Behind the Scenes: Great Value Addition and Poor Branding

'Ideally, if you want to be a star, you should have a consistent record of delivery with the accompanying skills of a great consultant. And backing it up, you need a strong network, a presence in industry events and media coverage within industry circles. Those successful at building their brand are quoted on important domain-related aspects in the media. Your personality and outlook towards branding should also be well aligned.

'The "Behind the Scenes" partners are loved by their clients and internal stakeholders. They don't seek the limelight like their "Hollow" counterparts. They find satisfaction in the value they create and have little interest in what the outside world thinks. They're happy to follow the other leaders in the firm without desiring a title of their own.

'I'm sure nobody wants to become "Hollow", and it's surprising to think that anyone at Pinnacle would fall into this category. But they exist, for one reason or another. Sometimes it's their insecurity, sometimes peer pressure or a need to impress the external world. Whatever the reason, they lose sight of their true priorities and stop contributing on a significant level. The most common result is that their team and peers feel they aren't adding value like they should be.

'At the end of the day, a partner has to bring value to the firm, as an entrepreneur does to his business. You, Samanta, have built a practice in Singapore and are seen as a good leader to your teams. You've brought your own value to the firm in your journey to becoming a partner. Now the question is how you can sustain your success and stand out among the other partners. You're among the odd 2–3 per cent who have survived the grind at Pinnacle and moved on to becoming a partner. So what do you think you will be bringing to the table?'

Samanta thought about it for a moment, but she already had the basic ideas in her head. She had been gathering her thoughts in this area ever since becoming a partner.

'It boils down to three things, I believe.

1. Business in my practice area
2. Guiding and mentoring my team
3. Being an ambassador for Pinnacle

'If I accomplish these, I feel I can really contribute to the firm and stand out among my peers.'

Ivan nodded. 'Those are all important areas to work on. But to take it a step further, you'll need to address a few issues.

The business environment is going to get tougher and clients want a better RoI. Competition is also getting stiffer and deals are becoming more difficult to strike. You'll need to learn to work with a much larger canvas and be able to influence both internal and external stakeholders at a deeper level. What's your plan to make that happen? You certainly don't want to be seen as a struggling partner.'

Samanta nodded. She had been thinking about the same things.

'I've thought of a three-pronged plan.

1. Leveraging the existing clients and building new ones
2. Creating more compelling proposals
3. Differentiating in the marketplace

'You know what I did in Singapore. Now I have the complete South East Asian and Indian markets in which to build my practice. I need to sell my story to other partners in the firm. They need to help me tell the story and educate our existing clients. I'm also thinking of partnering with analytics technology firms to align consulting with actionable solutions. This will help me differentiate in the marketplace.

'Also, our proposals are very good, but I feel the team needs to be on the same page more about how the proposals should flow for the practice. We received good training on proposal writing, but I take a bit of a different approach.' She listed her methodology for proposal writing.

'This is how it will go:

1. Start with an example of how our solution is going to help the firm.
2. Share the opportunity areas as we understand them further.

3. Explain the methodology of how we're going to accomplish it.
4. Explain the implementation plan—leveraging our partners if required.
5. Outline expected outcomes.
6. Present timelines and expected support from the client.

'Many of our new consultants mix these up. While we have our repertoire of proposals, making the proposal look like we've made it especially for the client is important. As a partner, I feel the critical elements are reviewing the proposal thoroughly and using it to convey a compelling story to the client.

'The other thing I've observed about proposals is that each client has their own requirements. Some like the proposal to be exhaustive, with detailed steps. Some want to see the big picture. Others want more case studies. All of this means we have to pick and choose our approach, depending on the needs of the clients.'

A recent experience came to her mind.

'Just a few weeks ago, I accompanied another partner to a meeting to explain the analytics story to the CEO and CIO of a company we were working with. The partner introduced me and asked me to explain how we were going to help the company. I had done my homework and had reviewed it with the partner to make sure I understood our proposed solution in detail. I shared three scenarios where there could be an impact on the bottom line and how our solution would improve customer satisfaction, increase value to the customer and also reduce costs. They were impressed, to say the least. Looking back, I realize I've learnt this approach through experience.

'In Singapore, a partner invited me to share the practice with his client. I shared how analytics worked and the various areas it could impact. After I finished, the client felt the whole concept was theoretical and shouldn't be a priority in his company at that point. The other partner talked it over with me and helped me realize it was important to keep it simple and make the presentation more contextual to the client. He helped set up another workshop with the same client to educate them on the possibilities. I did my homework more thoroughly beforehand and, that time, when I presented the information, the client saw much more value in what I was proposing. Even the initial recommendations based on the analytics solutions helped the client.

'Collaborating with other partners is definitely my way forward. I need to have an integrated story wherever I go and help the other partners share their solutions with the clients.'

The Business Builder

Samanta wanted to gain more insight from Ivan. And she knew he could speak about the area she wanted to bring up next. She gave him some background before asking her question.

'Building a successful pipeline is an important aspect of business growth,' she said. 'While established practices receive as much as 80 per cent of their business from existing clients, I have to start building new clientele from scratch. For our client acquisition or new business to happen, we need to educate our clients and find ways to advertise and explain our solutions in various industry forums. It puts a lot of responsibility on my team, especially on me as a partner. This practice is also young, and I realize that the younger team members will be the ones able to leverage the most from it.

Along with that, they need to have a solution-selling mindset with the clients they interact with. The problem is, many of them are uncomfortable with selling—they think it isn't their cup of tea. How can I change that mindset?'

Ivan looked thoughtful for a moment, but then nodded as if he had decided.

'I've seen this before,' he said, 'and I think the solution is simple. Don't have them try to sell. Just have them follow the steps of selling.'

Samanta hadn't thought of it that way before, and she decided to use the idea to experiment with the team. Samanta realized early on in her career that if she were to helm the affairs in a consulting firm, she would need to be a professional who could also sell. This meant she should be ready and willing to sell the services the firm offered and put in the effort to learn the skills to do it. Through her own journey of developing as a partner, she had learnt the steps of selling quite well.

1. Getting the leads/opportunities for account mining
2. Creating an opportunity
3. Scoping the opportunity
4. Selling the proposal
5. Closure and contracting

The first step of getting the leads was not often seen as a consultant's job. Usually it was seen as the sales department's responsibility. However, in professional services selling, the job of selling is often done by consultants up to the level of partner. In Samanta's case, she asked the consultants on her team to have active conversations with various stakeholders and clients on the many solutions they provided. These conversations helped Samanta gauge the clients' interest, so she could move forward in exploring further opportunities.

This made it easier for the consultants as well, since they were simply sharing information and educating the stakeholders without an agenda to sell to them.

The second area was basically marketing, which, in consulting, boiled down to knowledge sharing through practice papers or research outputs. Samanta helped her team members become actively involved in researching and sharing the output information with the clients. This also established credibility and helped the client see the consultants as thought leaders. On top of that, the consultants were able to engage more easily with the client on various core issues linked to the research.

The conversations at senior levels to generate interest and convert that interest into a proposal required some exceptional persuasion skills. Samanta remembered a conversation she'd had with a client in which she'd elaborately explained the process of the consulting methodology. However, the client didn't seem to be interested. She had seen the method she was using work with many clients in her practice. However, this client was different. She tried sharing examples of how the solutions had helped other companies with better pricing and customer value creation. These 'success stories' generated a lot more interest, and she was able to discuss possible areas of collaboration with the client.

The third aspect can include catching a client's attention by promoting the credentials of the senior consultants and partners within the firm. More 'educated' clients also look at who is going to be responsible for delivering their work. They tend to look beyond the brand to find the best consultants to work with. While Pinnacle believed its methodology and past experience was what mattered, it also realized that a good sales pitch might have to include some exceptional consultant profiles to have credence with certain clients.

Samanta had learnt to train the consultants on various aspects of creating a proposal that spoke to client needs—whether it included methodologies, client stories or profiles.

One of the skills Samanta had developed over the years was her diagnostic instincts. She could sense what the client's root problem really was and align her proposed solutions accordingly. Articulating the problem and aligning the right solutions helped build credibility with the client. As Samanta mentioned to one of her team members, 'Diagnostics is a combination of knowledge, inquiry and observation.' During the initial diagnosis with the client, a consultant should be able to understand the situation—discovering the existing problem through the right questions and observing how things worked. Creating a proposal based on the diagnostics makes it much more relevant and contextual to the client.

Building a Compelling Proposal

A proposal is an important aspect that can make or break a business deal. A proposal serves multiple objectives. It can help to share the consultant's understanding of the situation and the problem, the approach they will take, the phases, the deliverables and the timelines, their capability and, often, the cost or the investment.
A typical proposal is structured around the following:

- Understanding the organization and the problem.
- The key aspects this assignment will address.
- The approach—various phases of the project.
- Why the consultant's organization is the best choice for this assignment (this can be positioned in the beginning or while discussing the capabilities).

- Key team members who will be part of the project, with timelines.
- Budget/investment.
- Appendix: often case studies, details of the different stages.

While Pinnacle had standard approaches and even templates to creating proposals, one of the aspects that Samanta understood was that there was no 'one size fits all'. Some clients expected a very detailed approach, some looked at outcomes and some focused on specific aspects of the proposal only.

It was very important to focus on the audience. Often, a project would have to be presented to many stakeholders, and it was important to understand what their focus would be. Initial presentations will give clarity to the functional and operational aspects of the proposal. The need and scope of the assignment would have to be very clear by then. The final sign-off proposal would be the key decision-makers' and this would be often very sharp and addressing the core questions they may have.

Samanta remembered a discussion with one of the co-founders of a large e-commerce firm. The meeting lasted only ten minutes and focused on three questions he had. The risk of such discussions was that if they were not making the right impression, the assignment might slip away. A good consultant should be able to gauge the audience and adapt the presentation accordingly.

Developing this diagnostic instinct is an important part of becoming a partner. The trick is to listen to the organization without judgement or preconceived notions. If the partner has not developed this instinct, the proposals will look out of place, the client may not see the value of the proposal and the team may not relate to the partner.

One of the most important aspects of professional services selling is value selling. Why would a client pay large sums as fees on an intangible service? The consultant is selling knowledge, but how does one ensure that the true value of that knowledge is coming across? Whenever Samanta made a pitch to a client, she would make sure to include the facts that the knowledge the client would be receiving were:

1. Scarce
2. Available through a unique combination of past knowledge, experience and methodology of the firm
3. Delivered by specialists in the firm

While competitors might try to do the same thing, Samanta knew there would always be one or two aspects in her proposal that would make it stand out. It was one of her secrets of winning. The relationship and trust she was able to build with the decision-makers, the effort to understand the client and their needs better, and the confidence she gave the client made a huge difference.

At the end of the day, a client is trying to reduce the chaos or uncertainty in a certain area of focus. Sometimes, they don't know where the journey will take them. That is why the firm that truly wants to win the proposal should be able to promise a reduction of uncertainty as part of its service.

An important question Samanta pondered on was why clients went with a large firm such as Pinnacle versus an expert consultant in the field. After all, there were many other consultants who also promised to provide similar services to the big firms. How did Pinnacle beat them? Samanta realized it was again the unique combination of trust in Pinnacle's brand name, its methodologies and past experiences, and the impressive profiles of its consultants. The brand itself helped Pinnacle get a foot in the door, but the true test of a consulting project was whether the firm completed the work well and on time, and the client referred them to other companies or provided them with additional work. It wasn't uncommon for a client to drop the name of the company it was working with among its stakeholders if the company was credible enough. At that point, highlighting the brand's reach and promise was always helpful. However, Samanta had seen time and again that if the brand and methodologies of two companies were almost the same, the client would go with the consultant they felt more comfortable with. This was where the conduct and competence of the partner and the senior consultants exhibited during the initial discussion was so important–it could sway a client's decision in their favour.

As Samanta embraced her new role as partner, she made it a point to consciously provide opportunities to her team members to be part of the various aspects of selling. Some of them became interested in the process and started learning the ropes of this new path.

Whenever there was a major win or client delivery, Samanta operated from a 'we' mentality. The togetherness in wins and excellent client deliverables helped the team have more confidence. This, in turn, helped manage some of the losses and poor client feedback.

Dealing with difficult, and even embarrassing, client situations was a common event in a partner's life. Samanta remembered one situation in particular. The project involved her heading up a large multinational's entry strategy into India. The principal consultant in charge of managing most of the project was having difficulty managing the client. The client's expectation weren't being met by the recommendations and insights the team was bringing to the project. The client repeatedly stated that Pinnacle wasn't bringing anything to the table that their internal team couldn't produce. It was a difficult situation. The team was having a credibility issue with the client, and Samanta had to step in. When she and the principal consultant met with the client, the client shared that the internal buy-in for most of Pinnacle's recommendations simply wasn't there. And the insights weren't in line with the client's point of view. Samanta sensed what was going on. The principal consultant hadn't built the right kind of partnership with the client up front, and now the insights from the data weren't matching with the client's values.

Sometimes the presentation of too much data, coupled with a lack of relevant insight, can be off-putting for the client. Samanta went back to the drawing board with the principal consultant and the team. She had faced similar challenges during her journey to becoming a partner and she knew from experience that it was doubly hard to regain a client's lost confidence than it was to establish it in the first place. Samanta had discovered three elements to getting it right the first time itself. These were:

1. Discuss aspects of your solutions with the right stakeholders. The client shouldn't be completely surprised at your findings. Sharing your recommendations with at least the stakeholders with the most influence and seeking their feedback will help gain you more supporters.
2. Think through every possibility and variable. The more involved you are, the better insights you'll be able to

provide. Question your own assumptions, along with those of your team throughout the process.

3. Be confident about what you're presenting. If you don't have confidence in your own solution, the client won't either.

As a partner, Samanta realized that she couldn't let discouragement get to her or her team when they experienced failure. She felt her true test of leadership was when things didn't go well. The team was watching her, she knew, and would respond to the situation the way she did. If she was encouraging and optimistic, they would put in extra effort to overcome the situation.

'Why would a CEO or a CXO of a large firm seek feedback from you or your team?' The question had been posed by one of the senior partners within the firm during the partner-induction ceremony. All of the partners present had ideas. After all, they had been working with clients for years. 'Our knowledge,' some said. 'Our expertise,' said others. 'Clients need to reinvent', 'Our methodologies', 'that CEOs trust us' and 'great research' were a few other answers.

The partner, who was a role model for many, paused before saying, 'A CEO with decades of experience in their industry will know enough to run a company. But they want to know about the organization and industry from a neutral point of view. They want you to be their voice sometimes, and, often, they simply want you to help them validate their decisions.' He gestured towards a corner of the room. 'One of you mentioned the need to reinvent. The game certainly changes every now and then. If you want to be on the forefront of consulting and industry, be ready to reinvent yourself. This means you have to be hungry for everything new—read the latest news and research in the industry and learn from others. The advantage of being in consulting is that you get to meet new people and different client contexts. If you want to be a partner others want to have a conversation with, stay up to date.'

Market Sensing

Opportunities for client engagements come from three sources. The first, and often the easiest, is current accounts. The second is referrals. The third is through creating opportunities in the market.

Account mining is one of the most important roles of a partner. An effective partner will be able to build relationships to understand future needs and then create ongoing projects that provide long-term opportunities for work. A caution here is to avoid 'account fatigue'. The consulting firm and the client may become fatigued, or less engaged, over time. It's important for the partner to bring fresh value to the client through new insights and solutions.

One of the main principles that Samanta adopted was to make the client self-reliant. This often meant providing recommendations, enabling the client team to implement and finally own it, making it part of their day-to-day operations. This often involved capability building and even adding talent that could support the new way of doing things. Samanta believed that, this way, the client would be interested in engaging with her and Pinnacle on new challenges, and give them the confidence that they were going to make a sustainable change. This often was easier said than done. It was like a great leader making themselves self-redundant through enabling others so they can seek higher challenges and responsibilities.

Samanta had worked hard to develop the necessary skills to build relationships with new clients in the market. A new practice she was developing was instrumental in honing the skill. It was something called 'dynamic sensing'. 'It meant having a broad view of the industry and the specific company dynamics, and using the insights to develop solutions. It meant being open to information and insights from industry experts, business news, research reports, industry insiders and peer consultants. With deep 'dynamic sensing', a partner would have the pulse of the business environment.

Samanta acquired a project with an airline's large sustainable business firm using this practice. Business and share-market news showed that the company, despite increasing its share, was showing lower profitability quarter after quarter. This triggered the thought that the company was possibly struggling to make decisions regarding profitability. Samanta set up a meeting with the top management to explore their challenges. She developed pilot analytics solutions to explore the various cost-related decisions with measurable benefits. This eventually led to developing an entire analytics strategy for the firm and building in-house capabilities with Pinnacle's support.

The Intuitive Leader

Consulting teaches one to be analytical, data-driven and structured in one's thinking. Samanta had mastered this art very well. As one grew in the firm, the ability to think beyond the obvious became an important skill. Deep expertise, previous experiences, knowledge from others and sensing of the client helped a consultant bring out recommendations beyond the obvious. As a partner, Samanta was involved more in practice-building, networking and engaging with prospective clients, and building the brand for the firm. Client engagement was becoming more strategic. She was relying more on her team, which was working directly on client problems.

Intuition is a powerful tool for any leader. In consulting, one should be able to sense whether one is going to win an assignment, what the real need of the client was, get a sense of the interests of each of the stakeholders, understand what the team was really going to convey, and whether the insights were good and going to make sense to the client.

Samanta sensed the power of her intuition during the pitch for a large assignment. There were four other firms in the fray. The Pinnacle team had put forth a powerful presentation to the client. The team felt that the presentation and client engagement were great, but Samanta could sense some unease with the strategy head, who was at the presentation. She had a hunch that if something was not done immediately, Pinnacle was not going to get the assignment. She sought a meeting with the strategy head to discuss some pointers. It turned out that he was not very impressed with the team. Though Samanta was its leader, the rest of the team members were not well experienced in this kind of project. Samanta was quick to work on it and put together another set of experts in line with the client's expectations.

Samanta started relying on her intuition more as she was on the cusp of becoming a partner. The feedback she had got that she was straight-jacketed was something she wanted to do away with. Her intuition helped glean more from data, think out of the box and also add that extra 'element' to her thought process. Samanta had two approaches to enhancing the intuitive angle:

1. *Seek the questions and you will have the answers:* It is important to think from the stakeholder's perspective. What kind of questions they will have will be an important aspect of what kind of answers are required.
2. *Seek beyond the obvious:* X leading to Y is the general hypothesis of any problem statement. However, there

are many variables that are involved and the intuitive brain helps to think beyond X and Y, and explore other variables. For example, in an assignment that Samanta's team did for the automotive industry association in India, the entire consumption story was showing growth. However, she was able to visualize the possibilities of regulatory compliance related to the environment, which could change. While the industry was anticipating it, the risks were not really spelt out. Samanta's analysis put forth the possibility that even a short-term fall in demand, coupled with changes in emission standards, could have a multiplier effect and lead to a steep slowdown. This was then later experienced by many players in the industry. This is an example of how intelligent intuition can go beyond the pure data-based approach.

The same intuition helped her gauge the possible acceptance of a recommendation to the client and explore possibilities beyond available solutions.

Dealing with Mistakes and Failures

A consultant goes through tough client situations—'avalanches' where the client is not convinced and the consultant kind of drowns in their questions. During those moments, either one deals with them or the partner who owns the account has a way out. It was in such moments that Samanta realized that a 'leader is made in the moments of failures and mistakes'.

As a partner, Samanta realized she was answerable to her team, clients and to the firm than earlier. There was also a larger ecosystem in the firm that comprised peers and other senior partners. In a hyper-competitive environment, everybody wanted to safeguard their image.

Samanta remembered an incident that happened with a new-age cab-booking platform. While the organization had a strong internal team that also comprised some former Pinnacle employees, Samanta got to know that the organization was looking at evolving a strategy to become profitable in the near future. Samanta and another partner who was leading the technology practice had the opportunity to share an approach to the strategy team at the firm. The team felt that Pinnacle could add value and the strategy head, who was a former Pinnacle partner, was also supportive.

Samanta and the team put together a plan to support the firm. It was well evolved and they brought in practices that had worked with similar platforms globally. The final presentation with the founder was scheduled for an hour. The young founder was impatient and Samanta got a sense that he was not very comfortable with the consultants. The founder was hands-on in the organization and felt that somebody who had never worked in such an organization would be using this as an opportunity to learn rather than add value. In his mind, the consultants lacked the understanding of a new-age fast-evolving organization. The meeting ended with a cold agreement that the Pinnacle team would work with the strategy team and create a test case to show its value to the organization. However, even later the strategy team was not very enthusiastic to work with the team.

These situations can make a partner and the team feel dejected. They may start doubting their own capabilities. At Pinnacle, many also advised Samanta that they should have approached the client differently. Overall, losing the opportunity to work with a unicorn technology platform gave the firm a bad image.

She reflected on why the failure might have happened. Maybe they over-relied on support from the former Pinnacle consultant. Or the team might not have got a good sense of the founder. Or maybe the team should have spent some time discussing its approach with the founder before presenting to him?

Failures and mistakes can happen in any engagement. There are two options. One is to brood over these failures and blame the stakeholders. The second option is to learn from them, seek better solutions and come back stronger. One of the most critical capabilities of a senior leader as a partner is to have that sense of balance and not be reactive. Bringing energy and passion to every moment despite setbacks is an important skill.

Execution Excellence

Over a period of time, Samanta realized that consulting assignments followed a pattern. After drawing up a contract with the client, the engagement typically has the following steps:

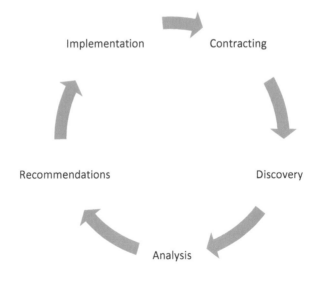

The initial phase is critical after contracting. Often, these are engagements with the senior leaders of the organization and it is about understanding the strategy, business challenges, practices and processes. Samanta realized that there were four levels of engagement managed by a consulting leader:

Client project team	The stakeholders who take care of the operations of the project. This is the engine that runs the project inside. They manage, coordinate, give relevant inputs and ensure the project is going in the right direction.
Client stakeholders	This is the team (leaders, external stakeholders, board members, partners) that influences the project and also provides relevant inputs and direction.
Consulting team	This is the team engaged in the project that needs guidance from the consulting leader.
Consulting leader	Motivating, learning and keeping the engagement going to meet its objectives.

Most of the clients like to see a plan of action in terms of execution of the project. Sharing the key action points, milestones, responsibility matrix and expected outcomes is part of the plan. The client project team should have clarity on what its role in the project is. One of the learnings that Samanta had was that no client project team had the same expectations in terms of its role. Some liked very active roles and even expected that their inputs would be taken in project execution. There are client project teams that just play the role of coordination and expect the consultants to do almost everything independently. Tools such as the GANTT chart and the RACI matrix help consultants give clarity to the client project team.

The GANTT Chart

This is a popular project-management tool that helps provide clarity on the following:

- Listing of various activities/tasks
- The start and end of the activities/tasks
- Which activities can happen parallelly and which ones are dependent on others
- Overall project-completion time

The RACI Matrix

This gives clarity on the various stakeholders of a project and what roles they play in it.

R: Responsible. The one responsible for the completion of a particular activity/task

A: Accountable. The one who owns a particular deliverable of the project (the sign-off person)

C: Consulted. Stakeholders whose opinion matters and inputs are taken to ensure a smooth sign-off

I: Informed. Stakeholders who need to be informed about progress and kept updated. They may not provide inputs on specific aspects of the project

Samanta remembered one of the toughest projects that she had handled—a six-month project to modernize the postal services in a developing country. It was a transformation project in terms of digitization and logistics optimization. Samanta was heading the project and had multiple partners and senior consultants working with her. To complicate things further, she had experts from across offices that were supporting the project.

The work of operations in the large postal services of the country was really complicated. She had to work with the top leadership of the department and government representatives, including ministers. It was a strategic project that promised efficiency and cost savings to the department. In a complicated system such as this, aligning stakeholders was a critical element to ensure seamless execution.

The team had experts who worked with some of the leading postal services. The team of expert consultants (supply chain, operations, finance and data analytics) worked together on understanding the challenges with the current system. Samanta suggested an interesting model of operations for the project. The operations of the mail system had five major hubs in the country. She wanted the team to have a thorough understanding of the operations and its challenges in one of the large hubs. The team also wanted to get quick results going on the project and adopted an agile plan that integrated client implementation with consultant recommendations. For example, if the team found out from its data analysis that the sorting of the mails was not appropriate, it provided the improvement suggestions to the client team and reviewed the progress of change within two days. Once the team could show considerable change in one of the hubs, the same would be replicated in the other hubs. There were also requirements of coordination between hubs, which were also addressed in parallel.

The postal services had gathered a high-powered team of ten senior professionals to support the project, who worked directly with the minister. This helped make recommendations work and approvals quicker. The team was also able to provide data-based dashboards on key metrics and how improvement in different aspects was helping the department. The team was also conscious of ground-level implementers. Even warehouses were restructured, both physically and operationally. From a visual that could be confused with a dumpyard, the warehouses started looking like well-structured assembly lines. This also helped the employees work better and faster, in a better environment.

At the end of the assignment, with apt recommendations and agile implementation, the project became a success for Pinnacle and the government client.

Some of the key learnings for Samanta in this project were:

1. Expertise is an important factor—involve the right team members.
2. Have your stakeholders mapped and involve them to ensure success. Build relationships based on expertise and communication.
3. Build confidence in the client by showing feasibility of recommendations at work.
4. Have a data-based approach to execution, with relevant trackers and metrics.

The Compass

Dealing with the top management, having a deep understanding of the organization, knowing potential upsides and downsides, understanding competition analysis and having access to insider information puts a consultant on top of valuable information. A consultant should be very discerning with this information. Using it for personal or business benefits should be avoided at all costs. Pinnacle believed this was sacrosanct and ensured that client information was shared only with the appropriate authorization and clearances. In the process of business acquisition or interacting with client stakeholders, often they would like to know about what was happening in the industry or with competition. Pinnacle guidelines were always clear 'the onus of the information is with the consultant'. This always created personal ownership with the consultant.

However, for Samanta, the compass was more than the process that Pinnacle as a firm had laid out. For her, it was about being true to herself, her team, the company and the client. Even accepting mistakes and challenges with clients helped Samanta in the process. Integrity with the clients and team was an important element of building credibility and trust.

As Michelle Obama says, 'At the end of the day, when it is time to make that decision, as president, all you have to guide you are your values, your vision and the life experiences that make you who you are.'

In a Partner's World, with Richard Rekhy

Richard Rekhy has more than thirty-six years of experience in management consulting and accounting. He was the CEO of KPMG India. He was also the COO of the firm and the head of KPMG's advisory services. Currently, he is a board member of KPMG Dubai. He has more than fourteen years of experience as a partner at KPMG. Previously, he was associated as a partner with Ernst & Young (EY), Arthur Andersen and RSM & Co.

1. In your experience, how does the growth from a consultant to a partner happen? What is the differentiating element that you see in a partner at a firm?

At the entry levels as a consultant, success is achieved mostly through individual excellence and partially through team work. As one moves up the ladder to becoming a senior consultant or an assistant manager, handling teams comes into the picture and one is exposed to the first level of induction into leadership. Further, as one becomes a manager, finer skills of managing projects, motivating teams, managing clients and delivering quality become important. At this level, one needs to focus more on managing multiple projects and clients. One also gets first-time exposure to business development. As one works with clients, there are a lot of opportunities to have conversations on enhancing the scope of the project or of new opportunities. As one gets promoted to senior manager or associate director, the role is an enhanced version of the manager—

more projects, larger clients and expectations on business development.

The next role, as director, means one has the potential to become a partner. Partnership, however, is a long-term commitment. There are many factors that help an individual transition from a director to a partner. Some of the critical ones are the ability to manage business development and collaborate across service lines, provide integrated solutions to clients, build and inspire teams, and have good networking skills. A partner is more or less like an entrepreneur. It is like building one's own business. Just as an entrepreneur, a partner needs to spend a lot of time in the market, seek opportunities to create a niche in the market and ensure there is a viable business and that long-term client relations are built. The most important quality is the ability to make an impact.

In my view, attributes such as high energy, hunger to do more, a genuine interest in people and living the values of the firm are key attributes to becoming a partner. They should lead by example. While the firm's brand is important, a good partner should be able to build a personal brand over time. In consulting, one who wants to succeed needs to follow their passion and not their paycheque.

There are some partners who can build innovative solutions and capabilities in the firm, which become a rare offering and often USPs of the firm in the market. These partners are valued for these attributes. The bottom line is that someone who gets noticed by making an impact has the potential to become a partner. They also need to have boardroom skills. A director who has not made it to the level of partner has not demonstrated business-development skills and the ability to make an impact.

2. Consulting is often a demanding career. How can one cope with it?

There are a few aspects of a consulting career that one cannot avoid. There is continuous physical and mental application. It is like being on a treadmill that is running at a particular speed all the time. One needs to run at that speed or get off. There are long hours, frequent travel, multitasking and a lot of time away from family. Creating a harmony between work and life is an important factor for having a successful career in consulting. It is important to destress, and find the time to keep one's energy levels up and one's body active.

Consulting is for those who have a penchant for learning, meeting new people and excitement about working closely with various businesses.

We have seen women representation in consulting going up. However, many of them leave in the course of the career due to the pressures of managing a family or better work–life balance. It is also interesting to see that the chairmen of top firms such as EY, KPMG and Deloitte in the US are all women. We will soon see this trend in India, as I see a lot of great female talent coming up.

3. How do you build great client relationships?

In my view, it is important to have a good understanding of client's needs and be completely engaged with them.

One needs to put themselves in the shoes of the client. Treat the client's issues as you would do yours and give them the time and the energy they deserve. One needs to build trust with the client. Having a trusted business relationship with clients is the best place to be in consulting. I have often gone beyond the terms of contract to ensure that the real needs of the clients are addressed. This involves making an effort to bring new insights to them and provide solutions to challenges they may face in future. Often, it is a trusted business relationship that gets built with the client based on the value that I bring to the table. In consulting, the client should hear from you what they did not expect—an insight or some data that will help them grow their businesses or deal with an issue in a meaningful way.

It is also important to know that everything may not go well. You cannot be oversensitive in consulting—you need to put your ego aside. Humility is an important trait. You should not feel bad when you get a critical comment from the client.

4. You have built a great network in your career. Can you give us some tips?

I love interacting with people. Spending time with people is something I always enjoy. In terms of building a network within the country and outside, I try and meet many people and maintain the connect once established. People and employees who reach out to me in times of need—be it personal or professional guidance or any other help—I go out of my way to build trust through action. People always trust those who support them in their bad times or when they were really needed.

I also attend a lot of industry forums. But it is not enough to just be physically present —you have to ensure your views are heard there too. It brings in a lot of credibility. Networking needs effort and good interpersonal skills. One needs to always add value. It is about making an impact. People should feel your presence in a room.

5. In the profession where disruptions are the norm, how can a consultant keep up with the changing needs of the industry?

I can say that almost every six months, a consultant has to reinvent themselves. To be ahead of the curve requires constant learning. If one stops learning or has a know-it-all attitude, it is very difficult to thrive in consulting, as the clients will be more informed than them. It is important that a consultant continue to learn new trends, concepts and practices. I would say reading, taking up online courses, connecting with experts, learning from peers and reflecting on learning from each of their client engagements help. It is important to always be a student and be open to learning from the environment. Reverse mentoring may be a good place to start.

6. What are some of your golden rules?

I believe in humility. Simplicity is something that makes one's communication effective and brings clarity of thought. Only if one understands something can one express it simply. Humility and simplicity also help you be at ease when working with others. I also bring a lot of passion and meaning to my job. Even making sacrifices on the monetary front for a great role has worked well in my career.

I am a strong believer in building teams. Essentially a lot of focus is on support to my team and collaborating effectively with others. This really helps. Carry your team with you, inspire it to believe in your vision and dream. Always look at the big picture.

It is critical to have your colleagues and clients trust you. Never do something that will undermine the trust that others have in you.

11

The Wisdom

It had almost been twelve years since Samanta had graduated from the Ivy League business school. She was nominated for the annual distinguished alumni award by her batchmates. It was a rare honour. The institute had produced some extraordinary alumni, and getting the distinguished alumnus award was something of great pride for the recipient.

Samanta was brimming with quiet confidence as she sat on the dais while the director of the institute gave the audience a glimpse of the achievements of the alumni who had been awarded that year. It was a dream come true. The director introduced her as a leader who had inspired many young students. He said that Samanta had made the institute proud with her achievements.

This was followed by a Q&A session with students, during which she shared her wisdom and experience with them. Samanta cheerfully looked forward to questions from the young audience.

1. *What do you think we should learn from the institute that made you so successful in your career?*
   Nothing beats a clear sense of purpose and hard work to achieve it. Develop the skills you can on the campus—critical thinking, teamwork, learning agility and discipline. Appreciation of the financial aspects of a business is an important skill to acquire early on. These can help you go a long way in your career.

2. *What are your golden rules of success?*

   - Believe in the Pygmalion effect. Your expectations from others will almost match what others can deliver.
   - Respond, don't react. You can choose how you respond. Have the will to manage your emotions rather than have the emotions control you.
   - Build your coalition. Build your network at the workplace and outside with those who will support you in your success.
   - Be the most passionate and energetic person in the room.
   - Be yourself. Develop your own style and personal brand.

3. *How do you sustain and grow in an organization such as Pinnacle?*
   In any organization, at one point, you may see that your strengths are not taking you forward any more. It is important to reinvent yourself then. The faster you are able to build more capabilities and do that, the more you will grow.

Learn from your failures. If we are not able to deal with failures and success with equanimity, there will be fewer chances for growth and change. Build a growth mindset and never let the feeling that you 'know it all' set in. Cultivated learning is the key here. Shed what is not relevant and add new feathers that will help you fly higher.

Never forget your moral compass. Trust and integrity are the foundations of a sustainable career.

4. *What has helped you be the adviser to the top management of large organizations?*

- It is important to build credibility as an expert and have the established authority in a field to be a true adviser.
- Knowing your client is crucial. It is important to understand the clients' needs and be ahead of them to be their adviser.
- Communicating with clarity and purpose is a key skill.

5. *What is your advice to the young consultants joining the firm?*

- Get a mentor or a coach. It is always helpful to get a different perspective about yourself. Have the humility to learn from others.
- Develop influence through performance, network and expertise.

6. *What is the one skill you think is important but difficult to find?*
Sales skills. It is an important asset as you grow in any organization. It is a combination of multiple factors—expertise, communication, networking and confidence.

An early orientation towards sales can help throughout your career.

7. *How do you think the consulting world is going to change in the next five years?*
The consulting world is determined by the client ecosystem. I would be ambivalent in my response to this question. There will be a spectrum of clients we are going to deal with. There will be traditional ones, which will require age-old approaches to solving issues. There will be new ones grappling with technology and digital transformation happening in their industry. I think there will be more of the latter, though.

There will be new tools in a consultant's kitty. Most of it will be technology and AI-driven. I would not be exaggerating if I said the solutions we are going to offer are going to be more technology-enabled. If the consultants and the consulting world are not going to change with this, both may become irrelevant.

However, the basic skills of a consultant will remain— the complexity and the technology angle is going to increase.

As Samanta ended her Q&A session, the director asked her a question: What is one critical advice you are going to give the audience?

'*Make yourself and others better every day*. I would say that sums up my career until now,' Samanta answered with a smile. 'Beyond self, team and the clients, I also contribute to the community. I have provided consulting services pro bono to five not-for-profit organizations that contribute to healthcare and education for the girl child. These efforts make one's life more fulfilling.'

There was a standing ovation from the audience.

Appendix 1: Campus Experience— Making It to Consulting

Straight from Management Campus, Aaditya Agarwal, Indian Institute of Management, Ahmedabad, and Bain & Co. Select.

The opinions shared have been gleaned from the lived experience of the placement process over the two years of the MBA journey—mine and my batchmates'.

Entry points to a consulting job

The students at IIM Ahmedabad (IIMA henceforth) have the option of joining a consulting firm in three distinct phases of their two-year journey.

The first route is through a summer internship between the first and the second year, which can result in a pre-placement offer (PPO). The second route is through lateral placement in select firms for students with work experience. And the final route is through the final placement process. Among the constellation of consulting firms that visit the campus, there are four that capture the maximum mindshare of students— McKinsey & Co., Bain & Co., Boston Consulting Group (BCG) and AT Kearney (ATK). These four firms come only for internships and final placements. Therefore, I will discuss the process in the light of these four firms during the summer internship (since the final placement process is very similar to this). But before that, I would like to dwell on the emotions that the idea of a career in consulting evokes in students.

Consulting Roles—the Dream

If one walks into the IIMA campus in the month or two leading up to the internship selection or the final placement process, it will not be uncommon to find hundreds of faces filled with anxiety or excitement at the prospect of getting a job in a top-tier consulting firm.

Like many others, I believed that these roles were the golden passport to help me reach otherwise-inaccessible career opportunities. There was excitement about the fast-paced nature of work, the travel, the chance to learn new tricks and tips of the trade, and the charm of working with extremely smart peers. It also felt like a stepping stone to future career options in the space of venture capital and private equity. To me, a consulting job seemed like a perfect finishing school to complement my two-year MBA.

These expectations were also set for me by my ecosystem, which included family members and friends who worked in these firms. I had first-hand seen the development in their communication skills and the opportunities they received after a few years in consulting roles. This enhanced my desire to take up one of these roles.

Internship Selection Process

The internship interview process typically happens in the last week of October or the first week of November. However, the groundwork for it is laid out by all stakeholders—the firms, the students and the institute—from many months prior. The companies usually come to campus in August to present a pre-placement talk (PPT). I remember the excitement that permeated the campus for a PPT from these firms. All students became part of six-member groups who internally decided among themselves who would attend which PPT. I had to request, and on one occasion beg, one of my group mates to let me go to the PPT from one of these firms, so I could get a better sense of the firm and also because the PPTs were seen as a mechanism to create a good impression on the representatives of the firms.

The PPTs helped me clarify some of the doubts I had about the firms and cemented my aspiration to work in a consulting firm.

During this time, I also actively sought help from my PGP2s (postgraduate programme [MBA] second-year students), who had received PPOs from one of these four firms. These interactions were driven by three points—to clarify doubts about the process, or get some 'real' insights, especially negative aspects that the firms would not share; to get help, as the seniors conducted mock interviews; and, lastly, as an opportunity to network and get to know more seniors. This has been a long tradition, where the senior batches invest in the first-year (PGP1) students' career growth. Being on both sides of this journey, as a PGP1 and PGP2, this was one of the most memorable parts of my two-year MBA journey, because of the opportunity I got to know new people on the campus.

During this period, the PGP1 students also organize themselves in 'case groups', which are three–six-member groups, formed to streamline preparation through interview simulations. The case group ends up being an extremely interactive set-up. Each simulation has three roles being played—the interviewer, the interviewee and the observer. The idea is to make one learn not only while answering questions but also as an interviewer and an observer.

It was with some excitement that I made my six-member group. I wanted to make a group with the 'studs' (read the smart and studious ones) on campus, so that I had a great learning opportunity and, thus, could reach out to people even before the selection process had formally started in terms of shortlists. There were some hiccups as, at this time, some people asked me to be part of their group and I had to figure out a polite way to refuse them. But, all in all, the case group over the course of the month and a half not only helped me sharpen my case-solving abilities but also to control my anxieties and, in the end, gave me a chance to know five extremely motivated individuals in my batch—relationships that I still cherish. Given we were spending a lot of time together every day, roughly three–four hours, preparing cases that had the potential to negatively impact over MBA studies, we ended up dividing some elements of course work among us, where, after the case simulations, we explained to each other topics for the next day's classes to save time.

Coming back to the process, our first set of shortlists came out in the second half of September and continued until mid-October. I remember the two questions that were on many lips, including mine, during that time: '*Kab aaegi shortlist* (When will the shortlist be released)?' before and '*Kiski aayi* (Who got shortlisted)?' after the shortlist was released. I got shortlisted for three of the four firms I mentioned above and my aim then became twofold—to better understand where I fit in and prepare to get the offer on D-day.

The release of the shortlist leads to a flurry of activity led by the firms. Each firm allocates a recent alumnus (graduated 0–3 years earlier typically), who works in the firm as a 'buddy' to the shortlisted students. The buddies end up becoming a one-stop shop for all firm-related doubts and many buddies also conduct telephonic interview simulations for the shortlisted candidates. In this, I got extremely lucky, as I had buddies in all the three firms from my alma mater, IIT Delhi. I suspect the firms do the mapping based on the backgrounds of individuals. The common connect helped me get very comfortable with my buddies as I was able to clarify all my doubts with them.

Shortlist announcements were followed by two events by each of the firms, wherein the representatives of the firm come down to the campus. The first, typically known as 'Informals', has more recent alumnus in the firm, who meet the candidates in a classroom for a fun session. As the name goes, the session is designed to be informal and the intent is to showcase the culture of the firm and help the students find their cultural fit. The relevance of this event cannot be emphasized enough. It was this event that helped me narrow down my options from three to one, as I was completely enamoured by the culture of one of the firms, Bain & Co. I could see myself fitting in well and my motivation at that time was to prepare extra-hard to get into it.

The second event is a formal dinner held with the senior leadership of the firms—partners and managers—on campus premises, usually the lawns. We were seated formally in a group of five–six, with the chance to interact with two senior leaders from the firm, who had dinner with us. Since my mind was already made up, I was more interactive in the Bain & Co.

dinner than in the others, bringing to the table questions about career growth within the firm. Post the dinner, my resolve to be part of the Bain family was even stronger.

Interview Day

All the discussions and preparations culminate in 'C1', the day these four firms come to the campus for interviews. These are similarly structured across the four firms, involving multiple rounds (typically two–three with each candidate), with each round consisting of a case situation that makes up the better part of the interview discussion, along with a few questions on personal experience. While the length of the interviews varies across firms and may change over the years, the general format remains the same. The interviews are conducted by the leadership of the firm and typically require at least one partner to be positive about the candidate for him/her to be selected.

On the morning of that day, at 8 a.m., I was called in by BCG instead of Bain. For ten seconds, I was shocked and slightly sad because, while BCG was a great firm, it was not the one I had dreamt of being part of. However, my friends helped compose me and I went to the BCG interview with a determination to get an offer from there. As expected, there were two rounds—the first was almost entirely consumed by the case study I had to solve, while the second, with a senior partner, was a general discussion on my interests. I bonded with the partner quite a bit and remember feeling during the interview that BCG would also be a great place to work in. My mood lifted and my energy levels went back to what they were before the interview. At the end of the second interview, BCG was kind enough to give me an offer.

However, my developed affection for Bain overpowered my satisfaction with the BCG offer and, after receiving my first offer, I decided to try my luck at Bain, thanks to this flexibility provided by the placement committee of the IIMA.

The team at Bain was very welcoming and, given I had a BCG offer already, my interviews at Bain, in my opinion, were short, compared to my peers. The two interviews with Bain ended up as opportunities to find my place better in the firm and, at the end of it, I received an offer from Bain as well, which I was very happy to accept.

The next steps included a lunch with the team from Bain, followed by a happy evening, where, for the first time in months, I was completely relaxed, as I planned the rest of my MBA journey.

Internship Process

In April and May, the candidates have to pursue internships with their chosen organizations. The actual details of the internship vary somewhat across firms. However, one thing remains the same—all interns have to work hard to inch closer to the pot of gold at the end of the rainbow, the PPO.

This was the case with me as well.

While my orientation happened in Delhi-NCR, where I had my home too, I opted for the Bengaluru office of the firm as my home location. This was driven by a conscious choice of not having the pressure to head home every weekend, so I could focus on sharpening my skills over the weekends and also finish pending work, something I was worried about.

However, during our orientation, I was told that I would be placed in an international location—the Middle East. I was excited but also a little worried, given the sudden international exposure. This did seem like a dream come true, though— being a consultant and catching international flights every Monday morning.

However, the travel every Monday morning was more tiring than I had anticipated. But I soon learnt the art of sleeping during a flight, after which travel no longer was a point of concern for me. Additionally, whether in Delhi-NCR, Bengaluru or the Middle East, the firm put us up in fancy five-star hotels, which made sure all our non-work-related issues were taken care of.

I also got lucky in terms of my team. The team can strongly influence performance, and I was lucky to have a team that treated me as a fellow employee and not as an intern. Early on, I was given ownership of individual work pieces and even got the opportunity to interface with clients. Given the particular project was in an exciting phase, our work hours were longer than I had expected. But our team, especially my project supervisor and manager, turned to be mentors par excellence.

I learnt not only a smarter way to think through problems but also received tactical advice on how do work faster. But perhaps what I cherished the most were the life tips that the senior colleagues shared with me, especially around maintaining a healthy lifestyle. I remember on one instance, I was given a piece of work that was due the next evening, but I worked until 5 a.m. to finish it and send it to my supervisor. I was expecting glowing praise from him but received a reprimand instead. He told me that it was an unhealthy way of working and that he expected me to be smarter about maintaining a balance between work and everything else. This was but one of such experiences where I learnt important lessons from my team. While the conversations revolved around work in the day, there was no topic that we did not bond over after hours—ranging from TV shows to American politics.

The internship also had an extremely interesting aspect. At the end of the first month, all the interns were taken to a resort in Goa for the weekend, where, first, there was an evaluation by leadership teams on the performance of each candidate until that point and, after that, a complete holiday experience. This weekend allowed us to get a feedback about our progress and also to get to know our co-interns from different campuses and other seniors in the firm. It was a chance for us to dream about knowing those we met better in the years to come, and for colleagues to become friends—an important aspect of Bain culture as I saw it. Goa was not the only time we met others in the firm in a party-like atmosphere, given we had multiple Friday-night soirees in the two months. But Goa was the most memorable.

Towards the end of our internship, on our final day, we were evaluated again in our respective offices by the leadership team. The next morning, as I was flying off from Bengaluru to the campus, I received a call from a partner at the firm that I had received the PPO—it is difficult to describe the kind of happiness I felt at that moment.

Final Placement Process

Given I have never experienced the entirety of the final placement process first-hand, I will describe it as I have seen how the seniors have gone through it.

The final placement process typically happens in the first week of February of the second year. This process runs similarly to the internship selection process, except for some notable differences. At this stage, the shortlisting metric moves sharply towards the activities done over the two years. Some of the key things that make the CV stand out are academic performance, whether a candidate was offered a pre-placement offer or not, key positions of responsibilities held, participation and winning in various management competitions, and extra-curricular activities pursued in IIMA.

The timelines are shorter, compared to the internships. The shortlists typically come in the first two weeks of January. At this stage, the second-year students turn to their batchmates who already have a PPO, and their first-year juniors, who have recently concluded their internship process for preparation support. The students with PPOs also take part in the final placement process sometimes to aspire for a career in a firm that is different from the firm they interned with.

In the final placement process, the interviews on D-day are typically longer and the expectation from the firm includes a more mature understanding of business contexts reflected in the expectation of more robust case-solving.

The remaining process elements are the same as the internship selection process.

Concluding remarks

A job in a blue-chip consulting firm is a dream for many candidates in IIMA. Through institutional support mechanisms, assistance from the firms and the candidate's efforts, this dream becomes a reality for many. I was one of the lucky ones for whom it did.

Conversation with Awiral Gupta, BCG Select, and Vhosky Rajoria, Bain & Co. Select,
Indian Institute of Management, Indore

Why choose consulting as a career?

Awiral: I felt consulting would give me opportunities to learn a lot. I could work across industries and with some of the brightest minds in the country. I had an offer from an investment banking firm, but I chose consulting because of these factors.

Vhosky: Consulting was aligned to my strengths. I think I have good communication skills. I can communicate my ideas really well. Even during my engineering days, I had prepared for consulting interviews. The case analysis done during those days reinforced my belief that I could have a deeper understanding of problems. All these factors made me take consulting as a profession seriously.

How did you prepare for the selection process, and how did it go?

Awiral: I had an offer in hand from a well-known investment banking firm. However, with my interest in consulting, I had worked on various case studies. There are books available to prepare for case interviews. I practised a lot of case studies and worked with groups of students who had similar career interests. The other important aspect was to have a well-drawn-up résumé. It is important to have spikes in all major sections of the résumé—academics, industry/internship experience, projects undertaken, positions of responsibility inside and outside the campus, and extracurricular activities. A conscious effort to build your résumé will always help you get shortlisted and in interviews. There were detailed case interviews and a behavioural event interview (BEI). The case studies were all about how I structured the problem, and came up with possible hypothesis and solutions. For me it was to make it as simple as possible. In the BEI, they asked me about various situations and what behaviours I demonstrated.

Vhosky: I got selected for the summer internship at Bain & Co. and was later offered a PPO. Most of the preparation that I did during my engineering days helped me during the interviews. They had three case interviews. There were also interesting questions, such as, 'On a normal weekday, how many people enter a popular mall in a city?' I think we need to think on our feet and make the right assumptions. The other questions were on allocation of the R&D budget, strategy for a Fintech and a market share case. I had a very good experience during my internship, which eventually led to me getting an offer. I had interesting learning during the internship. These were aspects such as understanding the client needs, researching, collaboration with team members, deep analysis and working with clients across the globe. It is interesting how we prepared our research and sat together in a collaboration room and to discuss the subject in depth. These were really intense and interesting. After each project, the team sat together and discussed what we had learnt. There were times we would have to stretch ourselves work-wise, but the firm also valued work–life balance. The internship experience reinforced my interest in consulting.

How did the management institute help you in the journey?
Awiral and Vhosky: At the institute, we had many sessions that were taught using case methodology. This helped us think like a consultant. Some of the professors also shared interesting frameworks and methodologies to solve problems. The conceptual frameworks and case method of learning were some of the biggest takeaways apart from peer learning.

Appendix 2: Consultant Mindset Assessment

Skills	Competence Areas	Behaviours	Score (1-5) 1: lowest 5: highest
Knowledge	Problem-solving	Arrives at various hypotheses to reason the problem.	
		Is aware of the various approaches and frameworks that structure the problem.	
		Challenges assumptions and drives new insights based on data.	
		Has an intuitive sense about the right solution that adds to the data-based approach.	

	Learning Agility	Researches on latest developments in the field.	
		Pursues better approaches and has continuous improvement.	
		Seeks inputs and learns from others on various aspects.	
		Adapts and applies oneself to new situations with ease.	
Application	Pragmatic Solutions	Appreciates the unique context of the organization to structure the solution.	
		Is able to suggest the right solutions that address the root cause of the problem.	
		Justifies the solution with expected outcomes and the return on investment.	
		Goes beyond theoretical approach to provide solutions that work.	
	Adept Educator	Advocating the right solution to the client	
		Clears assumptions and biases of the client through analysis and data.	

		Facilitates discussion and drives the client towards the vision of change.	
		Demonstrates excellent communication and presentation skills.	
Engagement	Managing Self	Confidently shares his/her opinion.	
		Displays tact and diplomacy as required.	
		Manages ambiguity and stretches oneself to achieve stated goals.	
		Establishes high standards and goals for self.	
	Managing Team	Helps others thrive with their strengths and capabilities.	
		Builds trust through coherence of words and actions.	
		Encourages others to provide better solutions to client challenges.	
		Provides guidance and shares possibilities and insights.	

	Sales Skills	Creates interest with current and prospective clients.	
		Creates value proposition that meets the business demands.	
		Co-creates and evolves business pitch that differentiates from competition.	
		Builds deep relationships within and outside the firm and leverages them for business success.	
Total Score			

Scoring:

A score of 112–140 indicates that you have evolved skills.

A score of 84–111 indicates that you have good skills in many areas but there might be specific areas of improvement.

A score of 83 and below shows that there are areas that can be improved through knowledge/skill-building and/or experience.

Acknowledgements

Almost a decade of experience in consulting has helped me grow as a professional. Anyone spending a considerable amount of time in consulting will experience a similar transformation. I am fortunate to have worked with more than a hundred clients across industries and places. This book is the result of those experiences. I thank the clients who trusted me to be their consulting partner.

People Business and EY are the two consulting firms with which I've worked. They made it possible for me to experience some very interesting client engagements and work with extremely competent co-workers. My own mentor at People Business, Mervyn Raphael, managing partner, helped me discover and develop the various capabilities needed to become a proficient consultant. I would also like to acknowledge my friends in other firms who supported me with their insight and counsel.

This book would not have been possible without the insights provided by experts in the field. Marc Cosentino, author of *Case in Point*, Richard Rekhy, former CEO of

KPMG India, Riaz Hassen, managing partner at Colombo Leadership Academy, Shital Kakkar Mehra, author and expert in executive presence, and Egbert Schram, CEO of Hofstede Insights, were kind enough to share their expert insights and interviews for the book. Aaditya Agarwal, Bain & Co. Select and alumnus of the Indian Institute of Management, Ahmedabad, along with Awiral Gupta, BCG Select, and Vhosky Rajoria, Bain & Co. Select, alumni of Indian Institute of Management, Indore, shared their interesting stories of getting into consulting firms. I thank them for taking time out of their busy schedules to share their experiences.

Writing a book needs a lot of support and encouragement from friends and family. My batchmates and well-wishers from IIM Ahmedabad were a constant inspiration in the journey. I would not have completed this book without the support of the family—my wife, Dr Dhanya Gangadharan, and my two daughters, Isha and Aekta, who always believed in me. Dhanya provided me with the much-required motivation and support. My father, Professor K. Kunhikrishnan, mother Syamala T.C., and brother, Dr Sudeep K. Krishnan, always believed I would do a good job with the book. I thank them for having faith in me! I thank my in-laws, Gangadharan Nair and C. Nalini, for their wishes.

This book would not have been possible without the faith Radhika Marwah, commissioning editor of Penguin Random House India, had in me. She was the commissioning editor of my first book, *The Making of a CEO*. She is a constant source of encouragement and pushes me to perform at a higher level than I ever have before. I thank her for having faith in me.

This book uses a storytelling style to convey the various concepts I wanted to share, utilizing anecdotes, case studies and conversations. I want to thank Angelo Oliverio Jr and Prakash Poduval (Indian Postal Services), managing director,

Karnataka State Police Housing Corporation, for providing valuable feedback on the manuscript. Ujjaini Dasgupta, who did the copy-editing, did a brilliant job by suggesting pertinent changes and posing questions that helped improve the manuscript considerably.

To all my friends who asked, 'When is your next book coming out?'—here it is. I hope you find it helpful.

Last but not least, I would like to acknowledge the numerous airlines on which I flew (in the luxury of pre-Covid-19 times) as part of my job. They gave me extra time in the air and during layovers to organize my thoughts.

The story of Samanta and the expert opinions have brought together very pertinent skills that would propel anybody's career ahead. I hope this book is a source of reflection for readers, which will help them to realize their professional peak.